A CLEAR & SIMPLE GUIDE

Floating Alaska!

Planning Self-Guided Fishing Expeditions

Don Crane

Dedication

To my wife for her love and understanding
To my dad for being a special person

Acknowledgments

I wish to thank the past and present professionals from Alaska and all over North America who have dedicated their careers to protecting and enhancing our natural resources. Their devotion to conservation is unmatched and unappreciated; their overtime hours not reimbursed; their hours away from their families uncounted; their battles with agency and external politics never ending.

My appreciation to all of those I have been fortunate to fish and share a campfire with, to those who have been so generous with their knowledge, experiences, and humor. I would like to thank my brother Bill for being a good fishing buddy, steelhead fishing teacher, a patient fly-fishing student, and a novice book editor; thanks to longtime friends Chuck and Ellen Reichert, John and Janey Hines Broderick, and Bill deVergie for being such fun and reliable buddies on countless adventures. I am grateful for having two fine daughters, Kelly and Kerry, and a son-in-law David; three young people who respect and enjoy the experiences of the great outdoors.

I wish to thank Bill Haggerty for his computer wisdom and never-boring personality; to Jerry Wolfe, a good friend, for his sound advice; to Kim Koch of Frank Amato Publications for her editing skills and helpful demeanor; to Frank Amato, a dedicated outdoorsman, for believing in and publishing this book.

Most of all, I wish to thank my wife of thirty-nine years, Mary, for her devotion, partnership, and patience. Without her I could not have completed this project.

© 2004 Don Crane

ALL RIGHTS RESERVED. No part of this book may be reproduced or transmitted in any form or by any means, electronic or mechanical, without the written consent of the publisher, except in the case of brief excerpts in critical reviews and articles.
All inquiries should be addressed to:

Frank Amato Publications, Inc.
P.O. Box 82112, Portland, Oregon 97282
503•653•8108 • www.amatobooks.com

All photographs by the author unless otherwise noted.
Cover photograph by Larry Tullis
Book & Cover Design: Kathy Johnson
Printed in Hong Kong

Softbound ISBN: 1-57188-338-X   UPC: 0-81127-00172-9
1 3 5 7 9 10 8 6 4 2

Contents

■ Introduction 4

■ Chapter One: Preparation 6
Planning, Participants, Who and How Many Should Go, Selecting Your River, Estimated Expenses for an Eleven-Day Float Trip, Sample Itinerary

■ Chapter Two: Gear 14
Maps, GPS, and Compass, Camp Gear: Take or Rent?, Catarafts, Rafts and Air Charters, Rowing a Raft, Tent, Sleeping Bag and Pad, Cook Shelter, Camp Kitchen, Dry Bags, Clothes, Firearms and Bear Spray, First-Aid Kit, Cameras and Film, Personal Gear Checklist, Group Gear Checklist

■ Chapter Three: Camping 34
Campsite, Water Purification, Camp Fire, Sanitation, Trash

■ Chapter Four: Food 42
Taste, Nutrition, Special Diets, Types and Amount of Food, Food List, Sample Menu, Dutch-Oven Cooking

■ Chapter Five: Fishing 50
Fly-Fishing, Lure-Fishing, Waders and Boots, Taking Salmon Home

■ Chapter Six: Wildlife 60
Bears, Biting Bugs, Wildlife Watching

■ Chapter Seven: Miscellaneous 66
Common Sense and Good Judgment, Typical Day, A Special Morning on the River, Public Cabins, Sample Costs for Ketchikan Area Public Cabin Vacation

■ Chapter Eight: Sources, Resources, & Services 76
Commercial Airlines Serving Remote Alaska; Floatplanes, Raft and Gear Rental; Fishing Information, Alaska Department of Fish and Game, Department of the Interior, Bureau of Land Management; U.S. Fish & Wildlife Service, National Wildlife Refuge, National Forests of Alaska Public Cabin Information

Introduction

The Grumman Goose landing at the remote setting of Kisaralik Lake.

For many years my occupation and interests have put me in contact with sportsmen and women from all over the country. I am amazed at the number of people who have told me they wanted to fish an Alaska river, but felt they just could not afford it.

I have never booked a guided fishing trip with an Alaskan lodge because my work did not pay well enough for the number of trips on my wish list. I would like to be "catered to" at least once in my lifetime as well as the next person, but I have determined that I can make two or three separate self-guided float trips of twelve to fourteen days in length for the same cost as one week at a premier Alaska lodge. Our small group of compatible people can fish the same rivers as their clients or choose something even far more remote.

FLOATING ALASKA! PLANNING SELF-GUIDED FISHING EXPEDITIONS

Over a span of nearly two decades I collected a vast amount of information pertaining to fishing fresh waters in North America, with a considerable portion of this relating to Alaska. It soon became apparent that it took some effort to put an unguided Alaska float-fishing trip together because the information, although available, was in bits and pieces, scattered everywhere. There was not one source for the majority of the things I needed to know.

This book is a compilation of those tidbits of information in addition to other pertinent techniques and tips I have learned from exceptional outdoorsmen, who are also my close friends or family, on fishing trips to Alaska, Canada, and the western states. This book was written for those "blue collar" men and women who truly love and respect the resources we are all so lucky to have and enjoy, especially those who desire to fish and explore Alaska at least once in their lifetime.

You will notice that websites are referenced to a large extent in this book. This is because they are such wonderful tools that provide much of the information you want to know very quickly. Many websites give you the option to e-mail some questions or ask for brochures. I have found that Alaskans are very prompt with their responses. Websites were not in existence years ago when I was floating rivers in Colorado, while at the same time spending a small fortune in phone calls to Alaska requesting any information available. Learn to use the web if you haven't already done so. It is a tool that you can easily master to help plan your Alaska fishing trip.

Readers must understand that new businesses, with their accompanying websites, are constantly being created as the public's demand for recreation increases. Costs of services change from year to year, typically increasing. It is imperative that you know with whom you are doing business; understand exactly what you are paying for, and what you are getting in return.

The information in this book is not restricted to just Alaska. The tips and techniques can be used anywhere, even on rivers not far from where you live. Hopefully though, your dream trip to Alaska will materialize and you will be better prepared for that journey.

During the preparation stages of your venture you will find yourself getting excited, and maybe a little anxious, at the thought of what you are about to do. While on your self-guided Alaska river float trip you will share, with your group, feelings of exhilaration and independence. At the end of your journey all of you will have the feeling of satisfaction; that you can accomplish an undertaking without being guided every step of the way.

Go and enjoy our forty-ninth state. Alaska is truly as great as it is reputed to be.

Don Crane,
Cody, Wyoming

CHAPTER ONE

Preparation

An overcast afternoon north of Bristol Bay.

Planning

A self-guided Alaskan float/fishing trip is not something you can throw together at the last minute and expect to work without flaws. Proper research, planning, and scheduling take time, at least six or eight months or more if you expect to have an enjoyable vacation. Can I afford it? With whom do I go? Where do we go? Where do we get reliable information? What equipment do we need? Am I up to it? Through a little research, a few contacts with professionals, and some additional reading, you should be able to answer these and many other questions. You then can decide if this is the type of an outdoor experience you would like to have.

I like to write down information, make lists and read pertinent guide or resource books. I also have phone conversations with appropriate fisheries biologists, refuge managers, Bureau of Land Management and U.S. Forest personnel. It is best to talk directly with the owner/operators of air charter companies to obtain specifics of their services, to determine their knowledge of a particular river. I also collect useful published information from state and federal natural resource agencies. All of this collected verbal and

FLOATING ALASKA! PLANNING SELF-GUIDED FISHING EXPEDITIONS

written information is then filed for future reference. You should select a person from your group who has good organizational skills, one who pays attention to details to do this job.

Communication within your group is vitally important. Everyone must be updated with any new developments or changes while always having an equal vote in any disputed matter. Get your group together every month or so, or at least have conference calls. Go over every minute detail from flights to food to make sure that everyone is on the same page. Spread out the preparation workload as much as possible by having each person be responsible for a certain task. One can acquire maps, another for purchasing dehydrated foods, the third for rounding up the cooking gear, and so on. You get the idea. Have a last group meeting or conference call a couple of days before departing to make sure all the details are in place and that all of the necessary gear is packed. There should be few if any surprises on your float trip if everyone participates in the planning process. Keep an accurate list of all expenses that occur before and during the trip. Do the math at trip's end to ensure that each pays his/her fair share.

Get your group together after your Alaskan vacation to swap photos and to view slides and/or videos. This would be a great time to begin planning your next float trip.

Participants – Who and How Many Should Go

Who should I Invite? What a hard decision to make! There will always be a friend or relative that will feel slighted because he or she was not invited for one reason or another. This may be the most difficult part of putting an Alaskan float/fishing trip together.

Let's start with whom. Obviously you want people who are compatible, easy going, fun to be with, dependable, stable, and who display good common sense. I hope that everyone has not been eliminated, but remember that your party will be together for a week or more in some very remote and wild country. Participants should also have basic wilderness skills along with some river rafting experience. They need to be comfortable on moving waters, around wildlife, and in secluded surroundings. Also, this is not a trip for someone with a serious health problem. Rowing, fishing, camping, hiking, and relaxing are not terribly strenuous, but "Flight For Life" is not just five minutes away, either. You also want people who will hold up their end of the workload, not be there just to fish. People will most likely find their niche after the first couple of days out. Some will prefer to cook while others like washing dishes or performing other chores.

How many? There are variables that ultimately will determine this number, but I recommend a minimum of two people and a maximum of six. Never, ever go solo! Three people are even better than two in event one person becomes sick or is severely injured and one person needs to go for aid while the third tends the victim. The number and size of available rental rafts can be the limiting factor. I would put no more than three people with their gear in a fourteen-foot raft or on a sixteen-foot cataract. Available charter aircraft can also be a limiting factor. Wheeled airplanes and floatplanes are chartered by the hour with each model carrying a maximum payload, anywhere from three hundred to eighteen hundred pounds. One of your first steps is to find out what charter aircraft are available for the particular river you have selected. A Beaver will carry approximately twelve hundred pounds, depending on the fuel load, while a twin-engine Grumman Goose can load up with eighteen hundred pounds. Calculate or estimate the weights of the people and gear. Match this total to the type of airplanes available. If, for example, the weight of your group with all the gear totals thirty-three hundred pounds, this load would require two trips by a Grumman Goose or three trips by a Beaver. A smaller-sized group might require only two or three trips in a Cessna 185. Plan ahead so you do not end up paying for a half-empty aircraft. Charter rates may seem high, but remember that these airplanes are very expensive to buy and to operate. Charter operators have a short season in which to make their businesses profitable. If your budget is really tight then you might find it less of an expense to have six in the party than four, or you can even choose a river that requires minimal flying time for access at the put-in location. Work with the weight numbers along with the charter rates and aircraft payloads on paper. Vary the number of people to find the cost that works best, then proceed from there.

Selecting Your River

The information in this book is intended for summer recreation in the Alaska wilderness. This would be from the first part of June through early September. Readers must take into account and be concerned with severe weather and icy river conditions during other months of the year. Even summer weather can turn foul in a short time and remain that way for several days. Before departing check river conditions with the federal land-use agencies such as the Bureau of Land Management, United States Forest Service, or the pertinent federal refuge.

There are hundreds of great fishing rivers and streams in Alaska that are also classified as floatable. Choose your destination carefully based on your river-running experience, river difficulty, wilderness skills, available time, budget, scenery, and quality of fishing. Rapids, falls, chutes, rollers, and waves are just a few of the characteristics of a river that determine its rating with Class I the easiest and Class VI the most difficult. For first-timers to Alaska I recommend a float that is from forty to seventy miles in length with a rating no higher than Class II. I suggest a minimum of eight days on the river, ten or twelve would be better, to allow for foul weather, hiking, good fishing, or just relaxing. Breaking down camp, packing the boats,

FLOATING ALASKA! PLANNING SELF-GUIDED FISHING EXPEDITIONS

Unloading the Goose at Kisaralik Lake.

then setting up camp at the end of the float day, along with the associated cooking chores, requires a considerable amount of time and effort. A trip shorter in distance but of the same duration will allow you to have multiple-night campsites near good salmon runs or close to mountains you want to climb.

Another important consideration, especially for fishing, is water quality. Select a small to medium-sized, clear-water river that is easy to wade and known to be a good fishery. Avoid large glacial rivers because of turbidity, wading difficulty, and the likelihood of poor fishing. A wide selection of available fish species is also important. Don't choose a river that limits your catch potential because it is sterile of fish except for one short salmon run each year. You might miss the run entirely because you were there at the wrong time. Look for a river that supports runs of at least three of the five species of Alaskan salmon in addition to a selection of other sport fish such as rainbow trout, northern pike, arctic char, steelhead, and arctic grayling. Cast a fly or lure into a good run on a high-caliber river and you may hook a six-pound char, a twelve-pound silver salmon, or even a fifty-pound king salmon, depending on the time of year you are there. A variety of fish species coupled with a few different fishing techniques makes for an exciting day on the water.

Dropoff at start of float. From left: Chuck Reichert, Kelly Crane, the author, Ellen Reichert, Bill deVergie, Mitch Copeland.

Any one of the following five rivers would be a good choice for your first Alaska river float:

Goodnews: 60 miles in length, Class I, floatplanes depart from Dillingham
Tikchik: 65 miles in length, Class I, floatplanes depart from Dillingham
Koktuli: 50 miles in length, Class I, floatplanes depart from Iliamna
Stuyahok: 50 miles in length, Class I, floatplanes depart from Iliamna
Alagnak: 66 miles in length, Class I/II. *Be sure you put in at Nonvianuk Lake, floatplanes depart from King Salmon*

I highly recommend *Alaska Fishing* by Rene Limeres and Gunnar Pederson. This outstanding book describes these five rivers in addition to most of the other floatable fishable rivers Alaska has to offer. You will find that it provides in-depth details about each river, including which topographic maps you will need and names and phone numbers of floatplane operators that provide service for each river. A second fine book is *The Alaska River Guide* by Karen Jettmar. Both are top-quality, comprehensive guidebooks that detail specific rivers, in addition to necessary things you need to know. These books are invaluable for selecting your river and planning your trip. Another book you will need is the *Alaska Atlas & Gazetteer* published by DeLorme Mapping. This is a book of topographical maps for all of Alaska to help you locate rivers and villages for planning purposes; it also provides helpful information about Alaska's resources. The Gazetteer maps are too small in scale to be used as your primary maps for navigation. The maps you will need on your trip will be discussed in a later chapter. Together, these three books will answer a multitude of questions.

You may think that this will be a once in a lifetime fishing trip to Alaska, but chances are this outstanding outdoor adventure will get in your blood, as it does with most everyone who has been there. You will want to go back! The memories of your first Alaska river float will stay with you. They will nourish your desire to select a more challenging and possibly longer float for your second trip. The knowledge you acquired from your first trip will give you an idea of what to plan for, who to contact, what is required, and what to expect.

Estimated Expenses for an Eleven-Day Float Trip

I will use the Goodnews River in the Kuskokwim Bay area of southwest Alaska as an example to estimate expenses for a float/fishing trip in the year 2004. This is a famous, world-class, sixty-mile-long river west of Dillingham that drains into Goodnews Bay. The following projected costs are for four average-size adults float fishing for eleven days in late June and early July at the height of the king salmon season:

Flight from Anchorage to Dillingham: $300.00/person	$1200.00
Floatplane (River delivery and pickup):	2805.00
Rental of two sixteen-foot catarafts: $70.00/day/raft	1540.00
Groceries and propane	400.00
Preship camping gear fees	350.00
Meals in transit: $75.00/person	300.00
Fourteen-Day Sport Fishing License: $50.00/person	200.00
Fourteen-Day King Salmon Stamp: $50.00/person	200.00
Tips & miscellaneous expenses: $125.00/person	500.00
Total	$7495.00

Note: Alaska does not have a sales tax.

Divide $7495.00 by four and the estimated cost per person is $1874.00, plus airfare from your home to Anchorage. The costs for this particular river trip could even be lowered if you could get by without pre-shipping your camp gear or you can fish later in the summer when a king salmon stamp is not required.

With a little research you can put a great ten-day float trip together that will cost each person a little under 1600 dollars including airfare from their homes in the lower forty-eight. A trip in this price range requires a river where the departure and pickup points are not far from where the float-

Ellen Reichert with a big chum salmon from the Kanektok River.

FLOATING ALASKA! PLANNING SELF-GUIDED FISHING EXPEDITIONS

plane is based or even a river that is not more than two hundred miles or so from Anchorage. Less time in the air greatly reduces the group's expenses.

Some of the more expensive lodges in Alaska charge 6000 dollars or more per person for seven days of guided fishing. It is difficult to find a good lodge that charges less than 4000 dollars for one week of guided fishing. Seven days on a guided river float will start around 3300 dollars per person. Airfare from your home, tips, and miscellaneous expenses also have to be added to the amounts quoted for guided Alaska fishing, whether this is out of a lodge or on a float trip. The Internet will give you an idea of fishing lodge prices with the services they provide. You can then compare costs between guided and self-guided fishing trips.

Sample Itinerary

Day One: Fly from your home to Anchorage; arrive Anchorage on late-night flight; find a quiet place in airport to rest.

Day Two: Take earliest morning flight available to Dillingham; buy lunch, licenses, remainder of groceries and ice, if you need it, in town; repack gear; fly out to Goodnews Lake; set up camp on lake shore; inflate rafts.

Day Three: Fish Goodnews Lake or Goodnews River or hike surrounding mountains; relax.

Days Four through Eleven: Float/fish the seventy-mile-long Goodnews River; camp, hike, or just relax.

Day Twelve: Break camp; float to village of Goodnews Bay; break down rafts; pack gear for return trip in floatplane to Dillingham; take last commercial flight available in the day to Anchorage; start home from Anchorage with late-night flight.

Day Thirteen: Arrive home some time during day or evening.

Note: It is important that you book the earliest flight you can get into the town or village, such as Dillingham, from where you will depart in the floatplane for your destination river to allow for bad weather delays. You should also book the last flight of the day to Anchorage on the last day of your float for the same reason.

Anchorage is a beautiful city with lots to see. Consider spending a day or two there to learn more about Alaska.

CHAPTER TWO

GEAR

Good tents are vital, especially during weather like this at Kisaralik Lake.

Maps, GPS, and Compass

Don't leave home without them! One of the first things you need to acquire after you have selected the river you intend to float is a set of topographic maps. These are the maps that show elevations, contours, drainages, lakes, ridges, valleys, mountains; they are loaded with the information you will need. The Alaska series that you will want are in the scale of 1:63,360. You may have to purchase six or eight of these to have complete coverage of the section of river you will be floating. At the same time you may also want to purchase a topographic map in the scale of 1:250,000. One of these may show the entire river system on it; it's fine for reference, but not good enough for navigation purposes because of its small scale. Topographic maps are available from the United States Geological Survey (USGS) in Denver, Colorado by phone at 1-888-ASK-USGS. First order a free Alaska Map Coverage index from the USGS, then use this in conjunction with the *DeLorme Alaska Atlas & Gazetteer* to determine which maps you will need. The two books I previously discussed—*Alaska Fishing* and *The Alaska River Guide*—also give a complete list of maps required for the river you select.

FLOATING ALASKA! PLANNING SELF-GUIDED FISHING EXPEDITIONS

Each 1:63,360 topographic map will have small light blue tick marks spaced about 5/8 of an inch apart around all four sides of the map. This is the Universal Transverse Mercator grid that is always referred to as UTM. The scale distance between two adjacent UTM ticks is 1000 meters. Most of the UTM tick marks will not have any numbers above them so look for one that does such as 6624000m.N. or 436000m.E. The numbers you find will not be identical to the examples here because they are all different, but this gives you the idea of what to look for. Use a long straight edge and a sharp pencil to draw your grid lines from corresponding tick marks from left to right then top to bottom across the map before you leave home. When completed, your map will have a square grid of penciled-in horizontal and vertical lines. You will also want to add the UTM coordinate numbers to each tick mark that was not originally printed with these coordinates.

You will now be able to use your hand-held GPS (Global Positioning System) receiver in conjunction with the UTM grid on each topographic map to determine your location within one hundred meters, or a little over three hundred feet. The Department of Defense controls the satellites and the accuracy of the navigation information given out by each satellite. The degradation of this accuracy is called selective availability or SA. You may find your accuracy as close as twenty feet, but anything under three hundred feet will work just fine on your float. Your GPS receiver will give you easterly and northerly coordinates for where you are standing at the time of the reading. You will then be able to use your special mylar scale to locate this position or point on your map by placing the mylar scale on the grid system you had previously penciled in. Your mylar scale must be the same as the map scale you will be reading which again is 1:63,360. You can purchase a mylar scale for about seven dollars along with other practical GPS information at www.waypoint-ent.com. To learn the capabilities of the GPS receiver, practice with this system at home before you go. It's actually quite easy and fun. You will find that it works equally well on all of your other excursions. Remember that a GPS receiver is a delicate instrument, thus it must be treated with care. I keep mine in a small foam-padded waterproof box along with the instruction booklet and spare batteries. The USGS also offers free publications on the use of the GPS system for reading UTMs.

You would also be wise to have an orienteering compass and the knowledge of how to use it. The Silva Huntsman is a small and inexpensive unit that is simple to use and understand. Take a bearing before leaving camp for a day hike over a mountain ridge. Carry your maps, GPS, and mylar scale; getting lost will be a thing of the past.

Don't get overly excited if the river features do not exactly match those on the map, because some of the maps are old. A tremendous amount of runoff each year accounts for topography changes along the river.

Your use of the GPS in conjunction with the map system will keep you informed of where you have been, where you are now, and where you will be going. This information will give you an indication of how much time you should plan for to reach your destination. Learn how to use these navigation tools.

Camp Gear: Take or Rent?

One important decision your group will have to make well in advance of your trip concerns camping gear. Do you take your own or do you rent? This may seem frivolous now, but it's imperative that all of your required gear be at the floatplane, ready to go, at the prearranged departure time. Floatplane operators have other charters scheduled, they cannot make expenses when their planes are sitting on the ground. Pilots can get a little cranky if they have to wait for you to get organized.

I know of several instances where people have checked in all of their camp gear at the airline counter as luggage. Low and behold, when they arrived at the small Alaskan village for their floatplane departure, their luggage did not unload off the same airplane. In fact, in a couple of instances, their gear never did arrive. These people were scheduled for a trip and were without camp gear altogether; they were indeed stuck between a rock and a hard spot. Needless to say, you can imagine their predicament of trying to roundup suitable tents, stove, cooking gear, and other equipment as well as rescheduling their floatplane departure time. Some groups even had to select a shorter trip because finding the appropriate camp gear in the small village took several days out of their schedule. If you plan properly, you can easily avoid this situation.

Several floatplane charter operators I know prefer their customers to ship their camping gear to Alaska about four weeks prior to the start of their trip. The charter service will store your gear in their hangar where it is ready for you when you arrive. This is a method we have employed and it has worked very well for us. We have shipped our camp gear in large, padlocked Action Packers to the charter service either by airfreight or UPS. One of us will phone about two weeks later to confirm they received it. To simplify matters, we always try to use air charters that also rent rafts. Upon our arrival we transfer our gear to his large coolers or dry boxes. We leave a clean change of clothes in the Action packers for our return home. The Action Packers work great for getting our things to and from Alaska, and on occasion we have taken them on the river. At the end of the trip, with space made available from consumed food, we have been able to take our camping gear home in the Action packers as luggage instead of shipping it as airfreight. This has saved us several hundred dollars in air cargo charges.

Because airfreight costs two dollars or more a pound to ship from the lower forty-eight to Alaska, it may be less expensive or more advantageous to rent your camping gear there. You can often locate a floatplane charter

FLOATING ALASKA! PLANNING SELF-GUIDED FISHING EXPEDITIONS

A medium Action Packer meets airline size requirements for luggage and is ideal for shipping camping gear.

operator who also rents camping gear or who works with a business in his village that does. Find out exactly what the rental costs are for the available equipment, then compare this with the cost of gear you would need to purchase plus the cost of shipping your gear to Alaska. These totals will help your group determine if you should rent or use your own gear. If you rent, you will still need to pack small items such as sleeping bags, pads, knife sharpener, rope, hatchet, bow saw, and other miscellaneous items that are not supplied. Rental equipment might also include cots and/or folding chairs that you would otherwise have to leave home because of their weight.

Remember that airline luggage regulations have changed. You are now allowed to check two bags that weigh no more than fifty pounds each, plus a carry-on that can weigh up to forty pounds. The lower limits make it more difficult to take all of your own camping gear, unless you are willing to pay overweight penalties to the airlines. It may be advantageous for your group to rent gear from a floatplane charter service or a company that works very closely with an air charter.

Catarafts, Rafts and Air Charters

Some people go super ultra-light on their Alaska river expeditions by using folding or inflatable kayaks or even canoes, but this is not the best mode of transportation for the majority of fishing/float trips. Catarafts or rafts with rowing frames are the standard for fishing/float trips because of their durability, handling characteristics, ease to fish from and carrying capacity. Be

Bill deVergie and Janey Hines Broderick are enjoying their ride on an eighteen-foot cataraft rowed by John Broderick.

sure that a spare oar is provided for whichever style of inflatable you decide to rent.

Rowing frames are essential on catarafts to join the two inflatable tubes as a complete unit. The lightweight, breakdown frame also serves as the support for the rower's seat and oar-lock system as well as a deck for gear storage. Two passengers can normally ride in front of the rower, which is an easy locale from which to fish.

Don't rent a raft unless it has a metal rowing frame with three good oars. The frame will give integrity to the raft and at the same time will allow for passengers to fish while one person is rowing. Paddleboats, which are rafts where everyone is using a canoe paddle, are fine for recreational floats such as sightseeing or whitewater day trips, but they are just not practical for a fishing/float trip.

Remember that all catarafts and rafts have load or carrying capacities. They will handle like a barge if you overload them. I recommend a twelve-foot raft or fourteen-foot cat for two people and a fourteen-foot raft or sixteen-foot cat for three people. An eighteen-foot cat will work for four adults if they are not heavyweights. Thirteen and one-half- and fourteen-foot rafts seem to be the most common sizes found in the Alaska raft rental business. They are just right for two or three average-sized people with their gear. Two extra-large people and their gear would require one raft.

You may find only one business in the small town or village you are

FLOATING ALASKA! PLANNING SELF-GUIDED FISHING EXPEDITIONS

basing out of that rents float boats, so you will have to take what is available. This is fine if the craft are in top condition and available in the sizes and numbers your group requires. Another option would be to have rental rafts shipped in by airfreight from another village or city.

I have met people who take their own catarafts to Alaska every year to float new rivers. On one of our floats we met two doctors from New Mexico who go to their same favorite river, the Kanektok, year after year. These are very experienced outdoorsmen who have their raft and camping gear systems finely tuned. They know the restrictions for airline baggage, plan accordingly, and use these limits to their full advantage. They take the proper-sized cataraft, breakdown frame, breakdown oars and the necessary camp gear. Everything they take is top of the line, but they only take what they need while leaving excess items at home.

I also know of a couple of guys from western Colorado who take their own one-man pontoon boats to a remote Alaska river every year or so. They carry all of their gear on the boats for extended trips. These men are able to float the smallest of streams where bigger rafts are not often seen. These are also outdoorsmen who truly have a great time doing something very few other people will ever experience. I have used and fished from small pontoon boats and found them quite enjoyable and comfortable. If I bought one of these to use in Alaska, it would be a ten-foot-long pontoon boat with eight-foot breakdown oars, a breakdown frame, and a load capacity of no less than 425 pounds. An inflatable of this size would not only work well in Alaska, but would be ideal for use on my favorite trout rivers back home. Buck's Bags, Outcast, Jack's Plastic Welding, and JW Outfitters make fine inflatables that meet or better these specifications. I am sure there are other brands out there that are just as good. Try your local fly-fishing shop or sporting goods store for pontoon boats.

You can find floatplane charters in Alaska that also rent rafts and camping gear. It is nice to work with these companies because you spend less time chasing down rental gear from all over town when you arrive. You will also want to locate a charter company as close to your selected river as possible to keep your costs down. Check references! Go with a company that is known for its good airplanes, staff, rental gear, and one that has been in business for several years with an outstanding reputation. There are many air taxis that meet these criteria. The following web sites will give you some ideas and information: www.pbadventures.com, www.fresh-h2o.com, www.aniakairguides.com, www.airguides.com, or www.brooksrange.com.

The United States Forest Service and the Alaska Department of Fish and Game have lists available of air charters as do most of the town and village web sites. You might also try www.outdoorsdirectory.com for a partial list of Alaska aircraft charters or find air charters for specific rivers in *Alaska Fishing* by Limeres and Pedersen.

The next step after you have selected your air charter is to book commercial airline tickets to the air charter departure town or village. At this time you will want to ask the airline agent for a lodge discount. Many air charters are on their discount list offering savings near fifteen percent. For example, this would mean a sixty-dollar discount off the normal four hundred dollar price of roundtrip airfare between Anchorage and Aniak.

Find out if a hand-held aircraft radio is available from the floatplane service or the raft rental company with which you are dealing. These radios are for emergency use only. You should rent one if available, but remember that they are only good when the weather allows airplanes to fly. The best option, if you can get your hands on one, is to take an all-weather operable satellite telephone.

I would be remiss not to mention other boat items that you will either need to rent or take with you. Each inflatable boat should be equipped with life jackets, throw bag, extra oar, air pump, patch kit, roll of marine or industrial-grade duct tape, one extra oar lock if available, bow rope, one or two small nylon tarps and boat straps. A large soft sponge is also handy if you are using a non self-baling raft.

Our group takes two or three dozen boat straps in four- and six-foot lengths. We strap each dry bag to the cataraft frame or raft behind the rower; then we secure a raft cargo net over this pile of bags and other camp gear. A nylon tarp lashed down to the raft over the stash of gear also works very well. This pile makes a comfortable spot for one of us to fish from or just to relax while enjoying the scenery. Our bow saw is always secured on the top outside of the gear pile in the event we encounter a nasty snag or sweeper. A sweeper is a low-hanging limb or log that extends over the river too low to pass under; for safety reasons they must be avoided.

We use a second nylon tarp on the front metal deck of the catarafts, in front of the rower where the passengers sit. This tarp prevents abrasion or other damage to our chest waders as we get on and off the cataraft to fish or stretch our legs.

Wash off any fish blood from the raft every evening, it cleans off much more easily when it's fresh. Also, remove any food or food scraps from your boat before you climb into your sleeping bag. I know of two people who woke up to find that their raft had been destroyed by a bear. They made the mistake of leaving food in the raft overnight. The bear can't be blamed because it was only doing what bears do best when they find some easy food.

Rowing a Raft

Rowing a raft or cataraft is an acquired skill. If you know the basics from the very first time you are behind the oars, you should get better each time you do it. Even if you are adept at rowing a small craft on a lake or pond

Sweepers can easily destroy a raft and ruin a float trip.

you will have to learn the proper methods of rowing down a river. The most obvious difference is that the rower on a river raft or cat is always facing the downstream where, from this position, he or she is watching for obstacles. The rower can then use the backstroke to avoid any dangers. This is just the first of many things you have to learn, to get adjusted to. There are techniques you need to understand and master to become a safe and proficient river rower.

Fortunately there is published information to help you. Rowing a raft or cataraft is almost identical to rowing a drift boat. Clackacraft is the manufacturer of exceptional drift boats. You can find four pages of text entitled "How To Row A Drift Boat" on their website, www.clacka.com. Neale Streeks has authored a fine book entitled **Drift Boat Strategies**. This is a comprehensive, yet easy to understand, book that covers the basics of rowing a drift boat.

The bottom line is that you, or someone in your group, must know how to row and handle a raft or cataraft. Seek out instruction from an expert prior to your river journey. It is a one-way trip once you start down the river. This is absolutely not the place to have an unexpected foul up!

Everyone should always wear a life jacket while floating even the smallest Alaska river. Hypothermia can set in very quickly from these cold waters, any time of the year. We have found Coast Guard-approved CO_2 vests to be quite comfortable, yet not overly bulky when fishing. Check beforehand with your airline to determine if CO_2 cartridges will be allowed on the airplane. If not then make sure standard life jackets are provided by the business that rents you the rafts. Be safe! Wear a life vest.

Tents

Wind, rain, or worse yet, the combination of the two, can discourage even the hardiest of fishermen. Your tent is your sanctuary, from dry, cool nights to the foulest of weather. The quality of your tent is of the utmost importance, especially if you expect it to last for more than a trip or two. Nylon tents are the most practical on a self-guided float trip because weight and space are critical. There are many fine tents on the market made by Sierra, Marmot, Moss, Mountain Hardware, The North Face, and Cabela's along with some I did not mention. Start with size. A four-person tent is actually just the right size for two people, plus their personal gear. A six-person tent is fine for three people with gear while being a snug fit for four people. An extra few pounds is well worth the added space, especially on an extended trip, so don't crowd your sleeping quarters.

Tents are like sails, and height is important. It is nice to be able to stand up to change clothes, but a seven-foot-tall tent in a fifty-mile-per hour gale can quickly flatten to the ground or even be demolished. Unless your tent is built like Fort Knox, the center height should be no more than sixty inches. Most fiberglass poles are extremely flexible. They will not stand as well as aircraft aluminum poles in severe wind. Since the poles are the frames of the tent it is important that there are enough to make the tent structurally strong. Three aircraft-quality aluminum poles should be the minimum, but do not use a tent that is overly complicated to set up. Make sure your tent has a rain fly that goes nearly to ground level on all sides of the tent. You will also find that a vestibule for gear storage is well worth the investment. Look at the Alaska Guide Model by Cabela's. It is a rugged, functional, and a quite popular tent made for Alaska's foul-weather situations. Use a ground cloth between the tent floor and the ground to protect the floor from unnecessary dirt and wear, but it is important that no part of it show from under the tent floor or it will trap rain water. You should also use another ground cloth or footprint on the inside floor to keep your tent clean and dry.

Bring something along, like a gunnysack, to use as a doormat. The less grit in the tent, the more comfortable you will be and the floor will wear longer.

Pack your tent daily in the cleanest, driest conditions possible. Also be sure to shake out and dry your tent thoroughly when you get back home to prevent mildew or other damage. With proper care a well-made tent will give you many years of service. It should outlast most of your other camp gear.

Most lightweight tent stakes do not do well in rock. The black plastic landscaping stakes, like those supplied with some brands of rolled rubber flower garden edging, are very durable and do not break nearly as easily as the commonly found cheap plastic stakes or bend like aluminum stakes.

Sleeping Bags and Pads

When the weather turns sour, you will be in your sleeping bag inside your tent on a gravel bar alongside some remote river for up to one third of your time, or possibly even more. For this reason you want your bed to be as comfortable as possible. Cots are superb if your tents are large enough and you can allow for the extra weight. Your other options are foam pads, inflatable foam pads, or inflatable air mattresses, but you want comfort with durability so try out the product before you go to Alaska. Remember to take the proper repair kit if you are using any inflatable pad. I like an oversized, extra-thick inflatable Thermorest, while a good friend of mine prefers two standard foam pads stacked one on top of the other. The days of cutting green pine boughs for a bed are long gone. This method should not even be considered.

Synthetic sleeping bags work best on river trips because they dry quickly if they should get wet. Add a flannel liner if you are a cold sleeper, but generally you will find that Alaska summer nights are mild. A twenty-degree bag is quite sufficient. Stuff the sleeping bag in a heavy-duty waterproof garbage sack or stuff bag; seal it tight. Always transport your sleeping bag in a stout dry bag.

A good down sleeping bag will work if that is what you own, but it is important to store it in a waterproof stuff sack. Be sure to pack it in the bottom of your dry bag at all times while you are on the water. Never let it get wet! A soaked down bag will remain that way for at least a week. Trying to sleep in a wet bag would not be the most enjoyable part of your excursion.

For some odd reason people do not take a pillow on a river trip. Some don't care to use one, but others, more often than not, just forgot to add it to the list. Pillows can be made in camp by packing a nylon gear bag with clothes or you can purchase a small stuffed model from a camping supply site such as www.campmor.com. My stuffed pillow is always on my gear list and has endured many trips.

Keep ear plugs in your tent so you do not have to listen to those of us who snore. You will want a restful and peaceful sleep each night because by then you will be pleasantly tired.

Cook Shelter

There is nothing better than sitting around the campfire with good friends or relatives after a long enjoyable day on the water. There's not much worse than attempting to cook and stay dry in a rainstorm for lack of a decent shelter.

We set up a cooking shelter on rainy and even on some cooler evenings to help make our camp more comfortable. We use a large nylon tarp with grommets for our group, sixteen feet by twenty feet is the minimum. You can use a smaller tarp for less people. Boat oars make great poles that are

Oars and rope make a great frame for a cook shelter.

even stronger than tent poles. Two oars are lashed together at the ends with boat straps to form an X, then a rope is half-hitched and strung between the X on each of the set of poles with the rope ends staked out to anchor each X. The tarp is then draped over the rope like a lean-to or sometimes all the way to the ground on both sides like a pup tent, if the weather is really sour. The back of the shelter faces the wind; use logs, stakes, or rocks to keep the bottom edges in place. If necessary, the shelter can be totally closed at the ends by using extra nylon tarps. It takes quite a bit of one-quarter-inch nylon rope to set up a cook shelter so be sure to take plenty. You can substitute the throw bag rope for the nylon rope as long as you do not cut it.

Dead trees or branches cut to the proper lengths also work well to build a suitable frame for your shelter. Never cut live trees for this purpose.

The best stakes we have found for our cook shelter were purchased at the lumberyard. They are twelve-inch-long round spikes three-eights of an inch in diameter. The spikes are a little heavy, but are indestructible and indispensable for very windy conditions. They hold extremely well in sand and gravel yet remove easily with a sideways kick or two from a boot.

One of the most important things to remember is that bears have a terrific sense of smell. Keep your cooking shelter some distance from your sleeping quarters. Also, do not put food of any kind in your tent. Even toothpaste, lotions, and shampoos have odors, so play it safe. Keep anything a bear might think is edible outside the tent, as far away as conveniently possible.

Take a folding camp chair for each person if you can manage the extra weight. You will appreciate their comfort while sitting under your cook shelter waiting for the rain to stop or around the campfire on calm evenings. Check with the business where you rented your rafts, often they have camp chairs for rent.

If a heavy wind rips off a grommet or tie strap from your tent or tarp, place a golf ball-size rock about five inches in from the edge of the nylon cloth. Fold the nylon cloth over the rock to form a small ball. Next make three or four loops of parachute cord around the base of this ball. Then tie it tight. Finally, run a piece of rope out to your tent stake where it should hold just fine.

Camp Kitchen

Our camp kitchen is very simple, efficient, and lightweight. We use a two-burner camp, preferably propane, and a Roll-A-Table as the focal point for meal preparation. Our pots and pans, including the Dutch oven, are all aluminum to save weight. We take Lexan plates, bowls, and cups along with heavy-duty plastic utensils. Our campfire grill is for boiling water or broiling salmon steaks. We take two collapsible water jugs for drinking water and cooking in addition to two lightweight plastic tubs or collapsible PVV buckets for washing dishes. A folding chair or two can always be found around the table; they are indispensable. Our cookware is stored in one large cooler or dry box while our foodstuffs are packed in another. We don't take ice, but easily could by taking another cooler. A lantern isn't really necessary in the summer because the Alaska days are so long. I recommend though, having a lantern for spring or fall trips, but make sure it uses the same fuel as the stove.

My friends and I have culled all of our camp gear from numerous hunting, fishing, horseback, and float trips in the western states as well as Alaska and Canada. Hopefully, what works for us will also work for you.

Dry Bags

To keep your extra clothes and sleeping bag from getting soaked on a river float trip, you will need a large dry bag constructed of PVC. The 3.8-cubic-foot Heavy Duty Bill's Bag is an excellent choice for this job. My sleeping bag, stuffed in its own waterproof bag, goes into the bottom of the Bill's Bag. There is plenty of room left for my sleeping pad, small pillow, clothes, wool sweater, Polar Fleece, and personal items. One-gallon freezer bags work great for packing socks and underwear along with quart-size freezer bags for toiletries. Extra shirts and pants fit in a lightweight nylon gym-style bag that also stuffs right into the big dry bag. Dirty clothes go into a heavy-duty plastic garbage bag that it is also stuffed into the dry bag along with everything else without any problems. The padded shoulder straps on the Bill's Bag are very comfortable. They were much appreciated during the many portages on a canoe trip with my daughter and friends to Ontario's Quetico Provincial Park. Although this is the dry bag we use, there are several other similar good bags on the market. Try www.downriverequip.com or www.nrsweb.com for dry bags and other specialty items such as one-inch-wide boat straps or collapsible PVC buckets. Dry bags can also be found at any good canoeing or rafting store.

A dry bag does not have to hang on a hook in the garage to be used only on river trips. Try one when snowmobiling, hunting, or hiking in very soggy weather. They work great. Where were they in our younger days?

Clothes

Take a close look at any good catalog today, and you can see how you could easily spend a month's salary on high-dollar outdoor clothing. Fortunately, this expense is not necessary to outfit yourself for a summer fishing trip in Alaska.

The most expensive piece in your clothing arsenal will most likely be a good-quality two-piece rain suit. The bottom line here is to stay away from the junk because you definitely get what you pay for. A three-day stretch of Alaska's wind and rain will make your life miserable when you find that your twenty-dollar rain gear is anything but waterproof. You will want packable nylon rainwear in lieu of the heavy commercial fishing raingear because of the weight and space requirements. Buy a size larger than normal for when you have to wear it over several layers of clothing.

Try to leave your cotton clothes at home; take wool, if you can, especially socks and long-sleeve shirts. Wear wool gloves in damp weather. You will find that your hands stay fairly warm even when they are wet. Cotton clothing is cold when it gets damp or soaked, it's not a whole lot of fun to wear in that condition. If you plan on wearing jeans, be sure to keep them dry by wearing waders or rain pants over them in foul weather.

I own down vests and jackets, but I don't take them on my river trips. They are very warm when dry, but useless when soaked. They take forever to dry out. Leave your down clothing at home for the cold, dry winter days.

My wardrobe for my Alaska float trips consists of wool socks, fleece pants, fleece pull over, polyester turtleneck shirts, wool long-sleeve shirt, wool gloves, polyester long-sleeve shirt, two-piece nylon rain suit, wool sweater, light-weight long john bottoms, wicking underwear, and a GORE-TEX waterproof cap. I can layer my clothing on a cool rainy day in Alaska

FLOATING ALASKA! PLANNING SELF-GUIDED FISHING EXPEDITIONS

Drying clothes and some of the crew (from left: Ron Reichert, Jon Untied, and the author) relaxing in camp on the Kanektok River.

just as easily as if I was cross-country skiing on a March day in Wyoming. The principle is the same and the method works.

Some friends bought nearly new, name-brand wool shirts, wool pullover sweaters, and fleece jackets at thrift stores and secondhand stores. Five dollars was not a bad deal for a barely worn Pendleton long-sleeve wool shirt. My two daughters grabbled up my dad's old wool shirts from his closet. They use them on every fishing trip. Look around to see what you can find. You do not have to spend a lot of money because you won't be in a fashion show. Nobody is going to care about fancy logos on your expensive clothing anyway. Your goal is be comfortable, stay warm, and remain dry.

To view a great selection of new outdoor clothing at terrific prices try www.SierraTradingPost.com. They sell the name brands at big discounts.

For an early spring or late-fall steelhead fishing you will need to pack heavier clothing. Alaska's weather can go from one extreme to the other in a very short period of time, but to keep warm you must plan and pack accordingly.

Firearms and Bear Spray

A firearm should only be considered as a defensive tool on your Alaska river float. The exception to this rule would be on a hunt, such as combining

A happy couple! Chuck and Ellen Reichert.

a moose or caribou hunt with your fishing trip. There are a number of Alaska fishing guides, government employees, residents, and visitors who have carried firearms for defensive purposes at all times when they were in bear country. Fortunately they've never had to use the weapon. There have also been a few unfortunate, unarmed victims of bear encounters who clearly wished for an adequate weapon at the time. You will have to decide whether a firearm should be a part of your equipment list. If it is, then learn your responsibilities regarding the weapon. If you take a weapon, then you must know how to handle it safely and be proficient with it before you depart. The firearm must be kept clean, serviceable, and always within easy reach while on the float trip. Do not put your party at risk by being incompetent with the firearm you choose to take.

Our group takes two Remington 870 pump shotguns with twenty-inch barrels and slings. The shotguns are always loaded with rifled slugs in the unplugged magazines, never the chamber. They are always readily available, whether in camp or behind the rower on each raft. We do not consider buckshot of any size effective for bear defense, thus we leave it home. Our high-quality, factory-loaded rifled slugs are much more potent than 00 buckshot. The shotguns are wiped down each evening with Hoppe's pre-lubricated gun cloths to ensure that the firearms are maintained in good working order. The most difficult part of taking a firearm to Alaska is keeping it dry. When the weather is damp, keep it covered, but keep it handy. Our shotguns also go into the tents every night where they are easily reached. Fortunately, we have never had to use these weapons for bear defense. I hope we never will!

Many people like to carry a .44 Magnum revolver in lieu of a shotgun or rifle when they are traveling in bear country. A short-barreled high-quality handgun such as a Smith & Wesson Model 629 with a three-and-one-half or four-inch barrel together with a good shoulder holster will suffice. Cor-Bon 305-grain Flat Point Penetrator ammunition is designed for bear protection; it's a smart choice. A word of caution, though: this ammunition has the recoil of a good mule kick. You would be wise to practice with it a lot before you go to get used to it.

I would not recommend anything less potent than a .338 Winchester magnum in a rifle caliber, if that is an option you are considering. Couple this caliber with 250-grain, pointed soft nosed, or partition ammunition and you will indeed have a very capable defensive weapon against bears. Contact your favorite gun dealer, he will gladly help you. He should be able to give you the right information about rifles, other firearms and even ammunition.

Remember that FAA regulations concerning the air transportation of firearms are very strict, especially after 9/11. Contact your airline well ahead of time to learn your obligations regarding your weapon. Know exactly what the regulations require before you step up to the airline check-in counter. You will have to declare your unloaded weapons; then they will be inspected. Special papers will have to be signed during this inspection. A maximum of two firearms per individual can be transported, but only in locked gun cases. The airlines will only allow personal ammunition with the amount usually limited by a set number of pounds or rounds. They will want the ammunition packed in its original factory boxes, in luggage separate from the firearm. This sounds a little complicated, but the procedure is not bad at all, especially when you know what is expected of you ahead of time. You will be required to abide by every written word.

Bear spray is another matter. Leave it at home unless you are driving to Alaska. Bear spray is pressurized; it will not be allowed on any commercial aircraft whether as carry-on, check-in baggage, or airfreight. Nor can UPS or parcel post ship it ahead of time. It will be seized at all airports. Check with your raft rental operator ahead of time to find out if he has bear spray available. If you are not comfortable with firearms, then you should consider the spray, even if you have to buy it, carry it, then leave it with someone in Alaska after your vacation is over.

First-Aid Kit

A small first-aid kit, packed in a waterproof container, stuff sack, or freezer bags, should be added to your list of equipment requirements. The following items are considered the bare essentials:
- 1 hemostat
- 1 small needle and thread
- 2 triangular bandages
- 12 bandaids
- 4 eye patches
- 3 rolls bandage gauze
- antacid tablets
- aspirin, Ibuprofin, Tylenol
- 1 roll white adhesive tape
- 2nd skin
- antibiotic ointment
- 30 antiseptic wipes
- 2 itch-relief sticks
- 1 small tube of Polysporin or yellow oxide of mercury
- 6 four-inch gauze pads
- 1 sam splint

Mosby-Year Book has published a small, packable book written by David Manhoff entitled *Mosby's Outdoor Emergency Medical Guide*. This is a good book to take because it covers all types of injuries and illnesses that may arise.

Cameras and Film

Everyone in your group should take a camera with extra film. If you are into photography as a profession or as a serious hobby then you most likely already own the equipment you will need. My advice is to watch the weight because a well-stocked, waterproof camera case can be quite heavy. Work out the poundage of all your photographic gear you would like to take *before* you leave home. Weed out any item that is more of a luxury than a necessity. This also applies to fishing, camping, and personal gear as well. Your baggage weight will be limited on commercial airlines and the floatplanes. You need to know what your baggage weighs before you get to the airport.

I ruined a nice auto-focus 35mm camera on an Alberta float trip years ago when the camera was accidentally submerged in the river. It would have cost more to repair the camera than to buy a new one, which is what I did. The manager of my local camera store showed me what he thought was the most durable and waterproof 35mm camera in my price range. It was the fully automatic Canon Sure Shot A-1 Panorama Date Pack. This is a tough, well-built little camera that has turned out to be as good as the

Bill deVergie with a spectacular Kisaralik River leopard rainbow.

camera store manager proclaimed. It is submergible down to five meters, gives me the option of taking standard or panoramic photos, has a built-in flash, self-timer function, and a quartz date function is available if I want it. The camera is light enough to wear around my neck all day while fishing or floating. I always keep it handy to take a photo of a friend with his big catch, spectacular scenery, or wildlife. This is a terrific piece of equipment that goes on every one of my trips. The great thing about this camera is that I never have to worry about getting it wet. Unfortunately this model is no longer produced, but they can be found on www.ebay.com.

There are several similar cameras marketed today. Carefully select the one that best suits your requirements and budget.

For film I use Kodak Gold 200 for color prints or Fujichrome Provia 100F for slides. These are excellent films that have produced for me in all kinds of weather and light conditions. Consider faster films if you are planning to take photos in very poor light conditions. Figure on using about six rolls on a float trip. After each excursion, I make a photo album that is loaded with my photos along with those that my friends took. It's fun to take out the albums and reminisce; this always stirs up the brain to start planning the next Alaska river float.

Hand carry your film through airport security. The large x-ray machines used to view the contents of your check-on baggage may ruin your film.

Ellen Reichert took her lightweight camcorder on a thirteen-day float that our group did in 1999 on a Bristol Bay river. This was an especially rainy expedition, but she managed to take and narrate a lot of footage while keeping the camera dry. Ellen later gave every member of our group a four-hour video of this memorable fishing/float trip that many people have enjoyed watching ever since.

There is one important item I learned years ago while taking a class from a professional wildlife photographer that I would like to pass along. He advised that the best wildlife photos most often come from focusing on the eyes. When the animal's eye gleams or shines while you are looking through the viewfinder, then it is time to take the photo. One word of caution though! If you are attempting to focus your camera on the eye of a bear, be sure you are looking through an extra-large telephoto lens while doing so. If you can see his eye through your point-and-shoot camera, you are much closer than you ought to be.

Personal Gear Everyone Should Bring

- ___ Sleeping bag
- ___ Small pillow
- ___ Canteen/or water bottle
- ___ Large plastic coffee mug w/lid
- ___ Wool sweater (pull over)
- ___ Small waterproof flashlight
- ___ Polarized sunglasses
- ___ Toilet paper
- ___ Mosquito repellant
- ___ Wool gloves
- ___ Sunscreen
- ___ Nylon packable rainsuit
- ___ Money, credit cards
- ___ Fly rods
- ___ Spinning rods
- ___ Flies
- ___ Steel leaders
- ___ Extra fly lines/tippet/leaders
- ___ Extra spinning line
- ___ Fly floatant
- ___ Chest waders
- ___ Wading belt
- ___ Sleeping pad
- ___ Large dry bag
- ___ Large folding knife
- ___ Shave kit & toiletries
- ___ Camera/film
- ___ Flashlight batteries
- ___ Whistle
- ___ Towel/washcloth
- ___ Headnet
- ___ Waterproof hat
- ___ Lip balm w/sun block
- ___ Lightweight daypack
- ___ Plane tickets
- ___ Fly reels
- ___ Spinning reels
- ___ Lures
- ___ Split shot
- ___ Needlenose pliers
- ___ Strike indicators
- ___ Fishing vest or creel
- ___ Wading boots
- ___ Knee-high rubber boots

FLOATING ALASKA! PLANNING SELF-GUIDED FISHING EXPEDITIONS

___ Personal medicines
___ Turtleneck shirts
___ T shirts
___ Underwear
___ Hiking boots
___ Waterproof matches

___ Wool socks
___ Polarfleece pants
___ Long-sleeve shirts
___ Polarfleece vest
___ Line clippers

Group Gear Checklist

___ Solar shower w/small tarp
___ Matches in waterproof container
___ Water purifiers/(1 or 2)
___ Hatchet
___ Knife sharpener
___ Ground cloths
___ Large nylon tarp for cook shelter
___ First-aid kit
___ Antiseptic wipes
___ Parachute cord
___ Duct tape
___ firearms
___ Hoppe's pre-lubed gun cloths
___ GPS unit
___ Roll-A-Table (1)
___ Camp chairs
___ 2-burner camp stove
___ 1 large cooler/dry box per raft
___ Can opener
___ Large cooking spoon & fork
___ Lexan Plates
___ Lexan cups
___ 12" Teflon-coated fry pan w/lid
___ Paper towels
___ Biodegradable liquid soap
___ Heavy-duty trash bags
___ 4' & 6' boat straps (12 of each)
___ Plastic 1/2-gallon pitcher w/lid
___ Emergency aircraft radio
___ Ear plugs (for floatplanes)
___ Nylon pot scrubber (2)

___ Folding army shovel (1)
___ Collapsible water jugs (2)
___ 18" bow saw w/extra blade
___ Filet knife
___ Tents
___ 12" spikes (8)
___ Fire starter
___ Biodegradable liquid soap
___ 100' of 1/4" nylon rope
___ Leatherman tool
___ Throw bags (one per raft)
___ Ammunition
___ Maps
___ UTM scale
___ Grill w/legs
___ Playing cards
___ Stove fuel
___ 10' light-weight wire
___ Spatula
___ Pot holders (2)
___ Lexan cereal bowls
___ Knives, forks, spoons
___ Aluminum Dutch oven
___ Dish towels (2)
___ 2 plastic dishwashing tubs
___ Hand soap
___ Boat tarps (1 per raft)
___ Action Packers
___ Signal mirror
___ Carabiners (2)
___ 3 nesting pots w/lids
(2, 4 & 10 qt.)

CHAPTER THREE

Camping

Plenty of fine gravel, windbreaks, firewood, and great fishing make this an ideal campsite on the Aniak River.

Campsites

Late in the afternoon as you float and fish you will want to start looking for your perfect campsite. Ideally this would be a sandy gravel bar on the lee side of tree line that will give some protection from the wind. The perfect campsite would also have a good supply of driftwood or dead wood nearby for your campfire. In addition to the above criteria, the ulti-

FLOATING ALASKA! PLANNING SELF-GUIDED FISHING EXPEDITIONS

mate campsite would also be located adjacent to a stretch of river that is loaded with salmon. Find a campsite like this and you may never want to leave. Each campsite you choose will provide its own opportunities for fishing, wildlife viewing, photography, hiking, and relaxing. Some sites will be better than others, but if you should come upon your perfect site then check your schedule. Determine if a two-night stay here will still allow plenty of time to travel the remaining distance of your float trip.

By choosing a gravel bar campsite you will be visible for some distance by bears. They are nearsighted, but they can see form and motion from distance. There is less chance of a bear encounter at a gravel bar campsite than one in heavy woods or forage. You do not want to complicate the situation by quietly walking around in heavy vegetation and surprise a sow with cubs or have a bear unknowingly walk down his favorite trail into your wooded campsite. Select a gravel bar campsite, keep it clean, and you should have no problems with wildlife.

Some of Alaska's great fishing rivers are located in tundra country where driftwood or dead wood is not available. This is where you will want to have plenty of fuel for your camp stove.

Do not carve your name or initials into bark, cut down live trees or even green limbs or leave any trash. Nobody wants to see names or initials painted or chiseled on a boulder or rock wall or broken glass, rusty cans, or cigarette butts strewn about. Treat each campsite and the entire river valley with respect, as if it is the most special place on earth because it may very well be.

Ellen Reichert with a nice Kanektok River silver salmon.

A great place to camp and fish on the Aniak River.

Another advantage of a gravel bar campsite is that high water each spring will clean the bar and renew it as if man never was there. This is not a justification for you to leave your trash or fire ring because this is inexcusable and should never, ever be done. Leave your campsite better than you found it. Totally police the area before you leave, pick up even the most minute piece of trash. The next group down the river will appreciate a campsite that has the appearance of never having been visited. Leave no trace!

Water Purification

Most everyone with any outdoor experience knows of someone who has had the intestinal disorder *Giardia*. I got it years ago from drinking out of a supposedly safe piped spring on a state fish hatchery in Colorado. I can tell you from first-hand experience that the symptoms are not pleasant. Beaver are a prime host for this protozoan. Alaska is neither immune to beaver nor *Giardia*. Do not drink untreated water unless you are willing to pay the price later on!

You can easily protect yourself from this nasty illness by treating all of your water with filters, boiling, and/or chemicals. We use a Katadyn Hiker filter for our drinking and cooking needs. Besides its large volume output, the model is easy to maintain in the field. It is an easy-to-use, very reliable filter.

There are several good water filters available. The Katadyn Pocket filter is an exceptional tool that will last a lifetime. The Pur Guide and First Need Deluxe filters are less expensive models that will work quite well for a long time. There are a lot of websites where you can find the filters; www.REI.com is a good place to start.

We also boil a lot of water, mostly for washing dishes, with a couple of drops of Clorox added to the rinse water for good measure. It seems that a pot of water is always on the grill whenever a fire is burning. We haven't found a purification tablet yet that we like because of the taste, thus we don't bother with them.

You can easily get dehydrated on your daily floats, or even around camp for that matter. Make sure you fill all of your bottles with treated water before you head down river each day. You might want to mix a powdered energy drink in some of the bottles. These drinks are more beneficial to your body than plain water.

Each of us used small personal bottles with a changeable filter on a trip we did on the Aniak River recently. Mine was the Outback model from

Bota of Boulder, and cost approximately $22.00. All I had to do was to remove the cap and filter, fill the bottle with clean-looking river water, replace the cap and filter, then squeeze the bottle. I had clean fresh water every time.

Consume a lot of liquids each day, but do not eat old snow from a mountainside. You can get very sick from bacteria by doing so.

A Dutch oven at work with water heating on the grill.

Campfires

A pleasant part of your Alaska camping experience is the evening campfire, but you need to know how to start a fire in rainy or damp weather. Take about one dozen fire-starting sticks that you can buy at most stores that sell camping gear. Two plumbers' candles are also handy. Your airline will not let you pack "strike anywhere" wooden matches, but you can get these when you buy your groceries in Alaska. Use a small bow saw to cut "dead" wood into twelve-inch lengths, then use a sharp hand axe to split these logs to get to the dry center core. Very carefully cut shavings with a pocketknife from the dry core. Next place about one-third of the fire stick, with a plumbers candle if needed, under the small pile of shavings. Add only split dry wood to build the fire for the first ten minutes or so until your fire is burning nicely. You will want to keep a supply of split dry wood under a tarp protected from the weather.

I have watched Native people jetboat up the river to collect berries on rainy days. One of the first things they do is build a small campfire to prepare lunch or to warm up. Fire is part of their culture and it can be part of yours if you follow these simple rules:

FLOATING ALASKA! PLANNING SELF-GUIDED FISHING EXPEDITIONS

- Build your fire in a sandy or gravelly location, well away from vegetation or soil
- Burn only dead wood
- Maintain a small campfire, not a roaring "white man's" bonfire
- Do not cut or burn any living trees or live limbs or peel bark from standing trees
- Do not leave an unattended campfire, for any reason
- Use plenty of water to douse your fire and stir it to make sure it is totally out
- Remove any unburned trash and foil from the fire pit, pack it out with you
- Cover the fire pit with sand and gravel and level off at ground height
- Do not leave a pile of unburned wood, disperse it
- Scatter any rocks you used around the fire pit

Sanitation

I previously discussed the importance of keeping and leaving a clean campsite. Dishwater disposal and human waste must be included in this category to make every user aware of his or her responsibilities while camping in Alaska or anywhere for that matter.

Use only anti-bacterial, biodegradable liquid soap for washing dishes as well as for personal hygiene. You can find it listed as Outdoor RX

Even the clear waters of the Aniak River should be treated before drinking.

A makeshift hot shower is far more comfortable than a cold bath in a river.

Outdoors Soap at www.REI.com. It is a concentrate, so a little goes a long way.

Thoroughly rinse all your dishes in boiled or treated water. A nylon scrub pad will be quite sufficient for your dishwashing needs. You can air dry everything if the weather allows. Dishwater should be disposed of well away from the river or any flowing water, the farther the better. Look for a sandy or gravelly area to throw out the dishwater, but try to avoid any vegetation while doing so. This also pertains to any water you use for shaving or personal hygiene.

During my career I witnessed many hunting campsites that upon first inspection had the appearance of being properly cleaned up. To my utter disgust, I would find an area of several hundred square feet behind camp in the vegetation that looked and smelled like the worst kind of latrine imaginable. Human waste and toilet paper would be above ground everywhere. The site would make almost any sane person sick to their stomach. The more I saw the more angry I would get because there is absolutely no excuse for this kind of behavior; it should not be tolerated.

Regulations on some rivers require portable camp toilets, referred to as "groovers" by seasoned river runners. This is especially true when the rivers flow through lands owned by Native peoples. Check the status of the river you intend to float; abide by the regulations imposed. Otherwise, you should use your small folding shovel to dig your personal latrine well away from any water source. Dig a hole in sand or gravel from six to twelve inches deep. Burn your toilet paper if you are absolutely certain your fire will only incinerate the paper, not the forest. Cover your latrine with the material you have dug; then let nature do its job of decomposition. Personal latrines used one time, then immediately covered, are much more sanitary and far easier to clean up than one large latrine for the entire group.

I cannot overstate the importance of maintaining and leaving a clean camp. We are just visitors, but the Native peoples make their livelihoods off these lands which are their heritage. For these, plus a multitude of other reasons, we must show respect to the people, and to their lands.

Trash

Your group will generate trash no matter what kind of food you take. The worse thing you can do is bury or leave your trash in this pristine country. The second worse thing you can do is be a bear-attracting trash scow that grows each day as you float down the river.

Do not take any tin cans or glass bottles. Prepackage your foods in freezer bags and wide-mouth plastic bottles such as those some powdered drinks come in. Buy your syrup, honey, and other liquids in plastic bottles in Alaska. If you want beer, make sure it is in aluminum cans, but remember that alcohol is illegal to buy in many Alaskan villages.

Burn all of your trash and food scraps at your campsite. Use your army shovel to remove aluminum foil before it melts. Also, sift the fire after it has cooled to remove any items that did not burn, place them in a heavy-duty double trash bag. This bag goes in the boat every day, not buried under dirt or rocks or thrown into the brush. Your group should have one trash bag, not much larger than a basketball, at the end of your float trip if you pack right and use these methods.

You might encounter trash left by a previous thoughtless or careless group—pick it up! Take care of it as if it were yours. It is far more enjoyable to set up a camp or fish from a gravel bank that appears like it was never set foot on by man than one that looks like a county dump.

CHAPTER FOUR

Food

Salmon steaks on the grill and a Dutch oven loaded with hot coals on the lid.

Taste, Nutrition, Special Diets

Most people have their own likes and dislikes when it comes to food while many have special nutritional or dietary requirements or allergies. For these reasons it's important that all of the group members are on the same page. In other words, everyone should get together several months before departure to work up a menu with a food list that's agreeable to all. If you have special needs such as a vegetarian diet or you don't like fish, let your buddies know well in advance of the float trip, not with a surprise announcement at your first campsite. Plan ahead. You may have to take your own foods if your requirements are vastly different from the rest of the group.

Types and Amount of Food

I know some guys, one of whom is a chef, who like three full squares a day on their river floats, starting with bacon or ham, omelets, pancakes,

FLOATING ALASKA! PLANNING SELF-GUIDED FISHING EXPEDITIONS

coffee, and juice. At lunch they pull their rafts up on a gravel bar where they break out the stove to cook up a hot lunch. Their dinners are major productions, equal to those found in many fine restaurants. If this is what you want, with time, space, and weight restrictions allowing for it, then by all means go for it.

Our group keeps the menu a lot simpler with less time required in preparing the average meal, yet we still experience some pretty fine eating. Our breakfasts consist of instant cereals, cold cereals, or pancakes. On special mornings we add hot biscuits with honey to the menu. Powdered dairy creamer tastes just fine on the cereals; we like it better than powdered milk and it requires very little space in the food box. We use packets of instant coffee or hot chocolate as well as powdered juice mixes. Warmed tortillas topped off with jelly or layered with a little liquid butter, sugar, and cinnamon make a great substitute for fresh pastries. Tortillas are very versatile, remain fresh, take up little space in the dry box; so, we take a lot of them as a substitute for breads with all of the meals. We can add bacon bits or fried fish to our breakfast menu for protein, but we don't take ice because of its weight. That eliminates fresh meats, except for fish, after the first day on the river for us.

Our campsite lunches include cup-a-soups, tortilla sandwiches, crackers, summer sausage, pepperoni, fish, and cookies, all chased down with a powdered drink mix. Aluminum packages filled with tasty chicken, turkey, and ham are now available at Wal-Mart and other large grocery stores. We use them for sandwiches because they do not require cool temperatures for storage. This menu will change somewhat for the days we are floating. Then we snack all afternoon on items such as trail mix, jerky, nuts, crackers, dried fruit, granola or nutrient bars, hard candy, non-melting candy bars, such as nut rolls, along with plenty of water or Gatorade. Each person packs his own lunches and snacks, usually in zip-lock freezer bags. This ensures that everyone will have the kind and amount of food he or she wants each afternoon for the entire trip. On those cold, rainy Alaska days, a small backpack stove set up on a gravel bar heats up a pot of water in a hurry for cup-a-soups, hot chocolate, or coffee. Be sure to have the stove, with the desired foods, packed on the raft where they are readily accessible.

Our suppers consist of a dehydrated main course such as beef stroganoff, mandarin orange chicken, enchiladas, or lasagna. Baked or grilled salmon or grayling sprinkled with lemon juice is, more often than not, included as a side dish. We also have soup, a vegetable, pudding, cobbler or cake from our Dutch oven, powdered drink, or coffee.

Dehydrated foods you can now buy are far superior to the old military rations. There is a tremendous variety available. We eat like kings while never going hungry. You can purchase complete meals that include entrees, vegetables, soups, desserts, and drinks. You may also make up

A CLEAR & SIMPLE GUIDE

Suppertime on the Aniak. From the left: Chuck Reichert, Bill deVergie, Mitch Copeland, Kelly Crane, and Ellen Reichert.

your own menu by buying individual dehydrated food items. This might be more appealing because of the vast variety available. There are several fine brands on the market that are easily found at good mountaineering, camping, or sporting goods stores or on the web. Try www.ldpcampingfoods.com to see a super selection of dehydrated foods, or to find items that are not available locally. A dehydrated pasta mix from your local grocery store along with an entrée, baked fish, and pudding makes for a delicious campfire supper. Health food stores are also a good source for dehydrated raspberries or blueberries for cobblers.

Your group must judge, well before the start of your trip, what your space and weight limitations for food will be. You must also decide on how much time you will want to take to prepare meals. Then you determine if ice, fresh meats, and produce fit within those limits or if the dehydrated foods are the better choice.

FLOATING ALASKA! PLANNING SELF-GUIDED FISHING EXPEDITIONS

FOOD

Remember that summer days in Alaska are long. You will be active most of the daylight hours and big appetites will be the norm. Prepare accordingly! Take an ample supply of food for everyone.

Alaska weather can be very fickle. It can change from good to very bad in just a matter of a few hours. It can also stay bad for several days on end. For this reason, take an extra two or three days supply of food in event foul weather prevents your pilot from arriving when scheduled. You might be at the pick up point for a few days longer than expected.

Food List

This is a basic list of food and items required for meal preparation that my group uses for our Alaska float trips. Items can be added or deleted to suit your tastes or even start your own entirely different list, but this will give you an idea of where to start.

Quantity

___ liquid butter
___ Wheat Thins
___ peanut butter
___ dried fruit, berries
___ bacon (for first morning)
___ pancake mix (add only water)
___ Swiss Miss (packets)
___ jerky
___ Gatorade (powdered)
___ dairy creamer (powdered)
___ salt & pepper
___ instant hot cereals
___ crackers
___ granola bars
___ beer (1/person/day)
___ Jiffy Yellow Cake Mix
___ cold cereals
___ honey
___ baking powder
___ summer sausage, pepperoni
___ lemon salt
___ heavy-duty tin foil
___ paper towels
___ Pringles
___ bacon bits
___ salsa & chips
___ Richmoor Complete Dinners for Four (dehydrated)

Quantity

___ coffee singles
___ tortillas
___ jelly
___ eggs (powdered)
___ syrup
___ vegetable oil
___ Cup-a-Soup
___ trail mix
___ flour
___ sugar
___ cinnamon & other spices
___ lemon juice
___ hard candy
___ gum
___ candy bars (non-melting)
___ Jiffy Corn Muffin Mix
___ Bisquick
___ hamburger or chops (first supper)
___ string cheese
___ nuts
___ garlic salt
___ zip-lock freezer bags (qt. & gal.)
___ cookies
___ pasta & sauce
___ raisins
___ instant puddings

Sample Menu

	Breakfast	**Lunch**	**Dinner**
Day 1			beef & bean burritos, chips & salsa, pudding, cookies, beer or juice
Day 2	cold cereal, juice, hot drink, breakfast rolls	soup, sandwich, Gatorade, cookies, dried fruit, jerky, chips	turkey tetrazzini, Sicilian mixed vegetables, cake, beer or juice, baked salmon
Day 3	blueberry pancakes, hot drink, juice, scones	jerky, trail mix, Gatorade, granola bars, dried fruit, nuts	chicken & rice, baked salmon, beer, raspberry cobbler, soup, deep-fried grayling
Day 4	hot cereal, juice, hot drink, cinnamon tortillas	crackers, sandwich, soup Gatorade, candy bar	mashed potatoes, beef & gravy, beer or juice, peas, cake, grilled salmon
Day 5	scrambled eggs w/bacon bits, biscuits & honey, juice, hot drink	soup, crackers, sandwich, Gatorade, trail mix, granola bar	spaghetti, beer or juice, strawberry cheesecake, deep-fried grayling
Day 6	pancakes, deep-fried grayling, juice, hot drink, scones	jerky, crackers, trail mix, cookies, Gatorade, granola bar, dried fruit	turkey supreme, chicken noodle soup, beer or juice, baked salmon, French apple compote
Day 7	hot cereal w/dried fruit, juice, hot drink, cinnamon tortillas	jerky, trail mix, Granola bars, chips, cookies, Gatorade, nuts	beef stroganoff, beer or juice, grilled salmon, blueberry cobbler, peas & carrots

Sample Menu

	Breakfast	**Lunch**	**Dinner**
Day 8	cold cereal w/dried fruit, hot drink, juice, biscuits & honey	soup, sandwich, candy bar, Gatorade, granola bar	lasagna, beef noodle soup, beer or juice, lemon pie, deep-fried grayling, corn-bread
Day 9	ham & cheese omelette, juice, hot drink, biscuits & honey, fish	sandwich, soup, crackers, Gatorade, trail mix, candy bars	cheese enchilata, tortillas, beer or juice, grilled salmon, cake
Day 10	pancakes, dried fruit, juice, hot drink, fish, scone	soup, sandwich, trail mix, Gatorade, granola bars, dried fruit	honey-lime chicken, green beans almondine, cobbler, beer or juice, baked salmon
Day 11	huevos rancheros, cinnamon tortillas, juice, hot drink, fish	jerky, crackers, dried fruit, candy bars, trail mix, Gatorade, nuts	beef stew, cornbread, beer or juice, pudding, deep-fried pike
Day 12	extra supply	extra supply	extra supply
Day 13	extra supply	extra supply	extra supply
Day 14	extra supply	extra supply	extra supply

The eggs with breakfasts are dehydrated. The other breakfasts are store-bought items.
Lunches are store-bought items.
Suppers are dehydrated except for some desserts and tortillas.
Take dehydrated meals for your extra supply of food.

Dutch-Oven Cooking

Nothing can please a person more on a river float than food prepared in a Dutch oven. Camp chefs have worked wonders with these simple cooking pots for decades. They have put smiles on the many faces that tasted their delicious recipes such as biscuits, cobblers, cakes, muffins, soups, stews, baked meats and casseroles.

The best Dutch ovens are made of cast iron which, of course, makes them quite heavy. Again, you are concerned with weight limitations. For that reason alone, an aluminum Dutch oven should be the choice for a fly-in remote float trip. It will work just fine. I recommend a ten-inch Dutch for three people or less and a twelve-inch for four to six people. Consider a fourteen-inch Dutch, or even better, two smaller ones for groups of over six people.

Briquettes are the normal fuel used to heat a Dutch oven, however, transporting a bag of these on an Alaska float is impractical. Use a folding army shovel to remove hot coals from the campfire, these are a good substitute for briquettes. A base of hot coals for the Dutch oven to sit on with one thin layer of coals spread on the lid is all that is required to transform this aluminum pot into a very productive oven. Wood coals won't burn as long as briquettes; additional coals will most likely have to be added during the cooking time. Don't get carried away with the amount of hot coals or the food will burn. Remember, you are working with an oven, not a blast furnace.

There are a number of fine books on Dutch-oven cooking. Start with your local bookstore. If they can't provide them, then it is time to get on the web. My favorite is *Cee Dub's Dutch Oven and Other Camp Cookin'* by C.W. "Butch" Welch.

The recipes that follow are intended to tempt your taste buds. If Dutch oven cooking interests you then give them a try, they're easy!

Basic Camp Baking Mix

1 cup flour
1/4 teaspoon salt
1 round teaspoon baking powder (try more at lower altitude)
2 tablespoons vegetable oil
1 tablespoon sugar

Stir up dry ingredients with a fork to work air into mix. Add a small amount of water to make a semi-thick mixture and then add the oil.

Basic Biscuits

Preheat greased Dutch oven. Tear off heaping tablespoon size chunks of Basic Camp Baking Mix dough and bake for 15 minutes or until golden brown. Eat them warm with butter and honey or jelly.

Biscuit Bread

Spread Basic Camp Baking Mix dough in a well-greased pre-heated Dutch oven without cutting dough into chunks. When the top is brown, turn carefully and brown other side. Split and butter.

FLOATING ALASKA! PLANNING SELF-GUIDED FISHING EXPEDITIONS

Scones

Stir 3 tablespoons of sugar into 2 cups of Basic Camp Baking dough and mix with 1/2 cup of milk or water. Add raisins or your choice of berries.

Pat out and cut dough into pie-shaped wedges and cook in a preheated oven with a small amount of grease. Turn when brown on one side.

Drop Biscuits

Mix 2 1/4 cups Bisquick with 2/3 cup of milk. Stir ingredients until you get a soft dough. Drop dough by spoonfuls into lightly greased pre-heated Dutch oven and bake for 8 to 10 minutes or until golden brown.

River Cobbler

(Dan Miller's recipe)

3 cups dehydrated berries of your choice (fresh berries if found near camp)
1/2 cup lemon juice
1 tablespoon cornstarch
1/4 teaspoon salt
1/2 cup sugar
A dash of vanilla
1 box Jiffy Yellow Cake Mix
1/2 cup Bisquick
1/4 teaspoon salt
1 tablespoon baking powder

Rehydrate berries with water to soften berries and create juice. Mix top items together and pour into greased Dutch oven. Mix cake items and sprinkle over filling. Dot with liquid butter and bake one hour or until golden brown.

Deep-Fried Fish

Filet northern pike or grayling and then cut into 1" chunks. Season with salt and pepper. Mix a heavy batter of beer and buttermilk pancake mix. Dip fish in batter then hot vegetable oil and deep fry until brown.

Oven-Baked Salmon

1 tablespoon liquid margarine or liquid butter
2/3 cup Bisquick
1 1/2 teaspoon parika
1 1/4 teaspoon salt
1/4 teaspoon pepper
3 pounds salmon filets

Melt margarine or butter in pre-heated Dutch oven. Coat filets with mixed ingredients. Bake for 15 minutes and turn filets. Bake until done.

CHAPTER FIVE

Fishing

The author doing some deep-water wading on the Aniak River.

Fly-Fishing

It's easy to overload the list of fly-fishing gear when you're headed to Alaska. After all, you will most likely be at least one hundred miles from the nearest town once you put on the river. There surely will not be any fly shops along the way to replenish your stock.

Three-, four-, or five-piece travel rods are far easier to carry on jetliners and floatplanes than are two-piece rods. They can also be packed inside locked duffels or dry bags while in transit through an airport as checked luggage. I have heard of expensive two-piece fly rods being removed from their cases after they have been checked in as luggage at the ticket counter. To their despair, the unlucky fishermen found the rods missing when they opened the tubes at the start of their float. I also know several fly-fishermen who lost all of their two-piece fly rods because thieves got to the airline baggage carrousels before they did. Consider insurance if you are taking a lot of expensive gear. Since 9/11 there have been changes in airline industry carry-on policies; check ahead with the airline to find out what is allowed.

As far as rod weights, a good-quality nine-foot five-, six-, or seven-weight will handle grayling, char, rainbows, and even twelve-pound northern pike or similar-sized salmon. I lean toward a seven-weight, along with an extra tip section, if I had to choose one rod for Alaska summer fly-fishing because it will cast better in windy conditions. A nine-weight rod, with luck, will work for big king salmon as long as the reel is well built, maintained, and holds plenty of backing. It would be better though, if you had a ten- or eleven-weight rod in your hands to tackle these monsters, especially when they are fresh from the sea. Large-arbor fly reels are now popular and a decent one can be purchased for around one hundred dollars, or you can spend up to six hundred dollars or more for a top of the line model. The Lamson Litespeed large-arbor reel is a very good choice. It is a dependable proven product with an excellent reputation. Your reel should have a good drag system; a disc drag is hard to beat, even by a big silver salmon. A loaded spare spool is also a good investment.

Fly Fishing Alaska's Wild Rivers by Dan Heiner is a fine book with loads of terrific information about fly-fishing gear and where to go. You should also check with your local fly shop. Tell them where you are headed and what your budget is. They will be very helpful, but try to buy gear that you can also use elsewhere, in fresh or salt water, for other species such as bass or bonefish. You never know when you will get an invitation for a fly-fishing trip to the Keys or Christmas Island. Quality fly gear is expensive, so don't buy equipment that sits in a closet and only comes out every ten years for a trip to Alaska. Thomas & Thomas builds some exceptional crossover rods which means you can use them in fresh or salt water.

Both floating and sink-tip lines should be included in your inventory. You will want a floating line with twenty-pound backing for your five- to seven-weight rod when fishing dries for grayling and mouse patterns for rainbows. Floating line also works well with most salmon patterns if the water isn't overly deep. A sink-tip line like the Teeny T-200 should be part of your fly-line inventory for your lighter rods. I like the Teeny T-300 line with thirty-pound backing on my nine-weight when fishing in deep water for larger salmon. Take along an extra fly line or two and backing. A big fresh king salmon might decide to head back downriver and strip your reel.

An assortment of tippet material in sizes 0X to 3X along with some nine-foot leaders in the same sizes will do the job for most fishing situations, but take larger sizes for king salmon. Alaska fish are not normally leader shy; you can generally fish heavier leaders than you would while normal trout fishing. Many Alaska fishing veterans prefer a very short leader tippet system, about three or four feet, when stripping streamers for salmon. They are very successful with this set up. Also, throw in a couple of short steel leaders if you are going to be in big northern pike territory.

You will not need to buy or tie up a hundred different patterns for your Alaska trip, but make sure you have a dozen or two flies of each pattern you know you will use. You will probably use and lose more of the salmon patterns than anything else, but still take a selection that will cover all fishing conditions.

The dry-fly selection should include some size 12 mosquitos, size 8 orange Stimulators, Adams', and Humpy patterns in sizes 10 and 12 for grayling and rainbows. Be sure to take some large mouse or mouserat patterns for rainbows.

Sockeye salmon can be very selective and seem to prefer skimpy flies. Here is a simple recipe for a good sockeye fly. Start with a size 4 or 6 chrome hook. Wrapped with lead wire and then wrap orange, chartreuse, or black ice over the lead wire in a Woolly Worm fashion. That's all there is to it.

Flies needed for salmon and that will catch about any of the available species, include the Flash Fly, Egg Sucking Leech, Popsicle, Babine Special, Orange Woolly Buggers, Chartreuse Woolly Buggers, Black Woolly Buggers, single egg, Polar Shrimp, Russian river. Decaying salmon and roe floating down the river provide plenty of feed for hungry fish; they often key on orange colors or pale crème colors such as the flesh fly.

You will also want a few nymphs such as the Half Back, Zug Bug, Gold Ribbed Hare's Ear and Beadhead Prince. The Zug Bug trailed as a dropper behind a Stimulator can be real effective for rainbows, especially in late summer.

Bring up www.hillsdiscountflies.com on the web to find a great

selection of flies. Jim Hill can provide all the flies you need for your Alaska trip at terrific prices.

If you tie your own flies, look at *Fly Patterns of Alaska,* available from www.amatobooks.com. Another choice is *Fly Patterns of Umpqua Feather Merchants* by Randall Kaufmann. Either book illustrates enough of the right patterns for you to fill your fly boxes for a trip to Alaska.

The majority of modern fly rods are made of graphite and even though they can be very expensive, they are still breakable. Many fly rods are broken when the fly is caught on a snag and the fisherman uses the old method of repeatedly yanking the fly rod with a continuous jerky arm motion. My brother showed me a method that works equally well with flies or lures while protecting the rod from breakage. When you know you have a hard snag, not a fish, wind in the line and point the rod directly at the snag. Hold the rod in one hand while grasping the line between the rod handle and the first ferrule in the other. Wind the line around this hand and pull then slack off several times. Be sure to always keep the rod pointed at the snag. Pull then let up on the line several times until the hook frees or the knot breaks. This method often takes the set out of the hook and the fly or lure will be retrieved with your rod undamaged.

FLOATING ALASKA! PLANNING SELF-GUIDED FISHING EXPEDITIONS 53

A happy Janey Hines Broderick and her beautiful rainbow from the Kisaralik River.

Lure Fishing

Two of my Alaska fishing partners, Chuck and Ellen Reichert, very successfully use a simple and inexpensive spinning rod setup on our Alaska floats. They use Mitchell 300 spinning reels loaded with 14- to 18- pound monofilament mounted on Eagle Claw Trailmaster combination rods. Their favorite lure is the 1/2 or 7/8-ounce Blue Fox Pixee spoon in orange on nickel color. They use a good quality 1 1/4" nickel swivel above the lure with a single Alaskan hook in place of the treble hook. Single hooks are required by law on many Alaska rivers; they do work very well. Chuck and Ellen have caught hundreds of fish on this rig, including kings up to fifty pounds. I recommend a heavier set up if you plan on going in June or early July for big king salmon fresh from the sea. Like fly rods and reels, you can also spend a fair amount of money on spinning gear. Again consider a three- or four-piece pack rod that will fit in your luggage, along with a good reel that holds at least 150 yards of line. L.L. Bean at www.llbean.com sells a very nice four-piece seven-foot spinning rod that

John Broderick with his first Kisaralik River rainbow.

handles fourteen- to twenty-pound monofilament. Sage and G. Loomis also manufacture top-notch, heavy-duty three- or four-piece spinning rods. Your local fly shop would be your best source for these. Have a spare spinning rod and reel in your arsenal of fishing gear in the event you lose a rod overboard or break one.

The Pixee spoon is hard to beat, but other lures that work well are large spinners in orange or chartreuse, 3/4-ounce Mister Twister type lead-head jigs in orange or chartreuse, and steelhead plugs in orange, blue, chartreuse, or green. My brother, Bill, has caught his fair share of salmon on popular steelhead plugs such as the Wiggle Wart in blue, orange, or chartreuse.

Don't scrimp on your swivels. They are just as important as your lure. Five-dozen swivels, along with a like number of lures, should be ample for a ten-day float. You can take less if you are also going to fly-fish, but count on losing some lures to snags and to big fish.

Clean, lube, and tune up any used reels you are taking. Be sure to inspect any new reel for loose screws or missing parts. Wind a fresh name-brand line on each of your reels before you leave. Lawn-cast all rods and reels before leaving to make sure they are in perfect working order. Pack at least 200 yards of extra new monofilament line for each reel, and a lot more if you are going to be hooked up with big kings. Be sure to protect the reels in your luggage from damage while in transit because a lot of weight will be on your bags going to and coming from your Alaska destination.

Waders and Boots

Two types of waterproof boots work well on Alaska float trips. The first is the familiar chest wader with felt or soft rubber-soled wading boots. I am a fly-fisherman who likes to wade so naturally I wear chest waders all day, every day. My three-millimeter neoprene waders suited me quite well on several Alaska trips; they were very comfortable. Another chest-wader option is the breathables which are now very popular with a large selection from which to choose. I purchased my first pair two years ago and have found them to be as good as advertised. Prices start around 150 dollars a pair and go as high as 400 dollars. Take your time when selecting your waders. You get what you pay for, including a warranty. Be sure to check your waders for leaks before you leave home and take the proper repair kit with you on the trip.

I wear polar fleece pants, which I really like, under my chest waders. Up top on the cold rainy days, I have on a turtleneck shirt, long-sleeve shirt, and maybe even a wool sweater under my waterproof wading jacket. Learn to layer your fishing clothing just like you layer hiking clothing. You can add or subtract as the weather changes. Make a habit of wearing a wading belt with your chest waders because it could save your life during a serious dunking. You can carry a can of bear spray, if you desire, on the belt along with a pair of needlenosed pliers in a small sheath. Some floatplanes will unload you in water two to three feet deep at your destination. The pilots will want you to wear chest waders on the flight because you and your friends will be wading to and from the shore, not the pilot.

The second type is the knee-high rubber irrigation boot. This boot works well for the spin fisherman who won't be in more than ankle-deep water or for around camp after you peel out of your chest waders. Buy a pair that is one size larger than you normally wear and use heavy wool socks. Your feet will stay warm and dry all day. You will be glad you brought them along.

Take these two types of boots with a comfortable pair of light to medium weight hiking boots and all of your foot/wader needs should be nicely accommodated. Try to dry out your waders and boots each evening, but be extra careful with them if you are near a campfire. They can be damaged or even totally ruined by sparks and heat. You are better off air-drying waders and rubber boots in your tent or hanging them upside down in the cook shelter for the night.

Be sure to sterilize any used rubber or wading boots in a Clorox/water solution before you leave home. You do not want to be the transmitter of whirling disease spores to Alaska's fresh waters.

Bringing Salmon Home

Bringing home fresh Alaska salmon for the grill will surely please your friends and family. These occasions also give you additional opportunities to brag about your fishing prowess while thinking about a future trip. Bringing fresh salmon home requires some luck and planning.

The luck involves the fishing. You will need to be in a situation that enables you to catch a limit of salmon on the last day or two of your float trip. You do not want to attempt to keep salmon caught at the start or even several days into your trip. It would be very difficult to keep these fish fresh and you are asking for trouble from bears. A cooler of salmon filets is bear bait, and an unnecessary encounter would quickly spoil your trip.

The planning concerns the ice supply on the float and freezing the fish before you depart Alaska. Ice will last for a week or more in coolers if you are very careful. The coolers will have to be opened as little as possible while being covered and stored in the shade at all times. Try duct taping the lid seams on a cooler that has only block ice in it, no food or drink, and only open the cooler when you need it. Block ice will last longer than cubes; water frozen in one-gallon plastic milk jugs lasts even longer than cubes or block ice.

Airlines will transport frozen fish, not fresh fish on ice. They will limit you to around four pounds of dry ice or you could use several of the

A nice leopard rainbow taken by Bill Crane on the Kanektok River.

FLOATING ALASKA! PLANNING SELF-GUIDED FISHING EXPEDITIONS

Jon Untied with a pretty Kanektok River rainbow.

sealed and frozen blue bottles. You will not be allowed to transport ice cubes or block ice on commercial aircraft. For this reason you will have to locate a processor that can quick-freeze your catch, but this process generally requires an overnight stay if you want to take the fish home as baggage. Some floatplane charters have freezers as well as waxed boxes at their hangars to prepare fish for transport for their customers. Another option is to leave your salmon with a processor in Alaska to have them shipped to your home at a later date. You will get your own fish with this method, along with a hefty airfreight bill. It might be a lot less expensive to buy fresh salmon from your local market.

Our group doesn't bother with trying to take salmon home, or even having ice on the float for that matter. We practice CPR; catch, photograph, and release. We are quite content to return all of the fish we catch to the water except for one choice salmon in the eight-pound class or a couple of grayling each day. This is part of our supper and we cannot get it any fresher than that.

You will have to make the decision on whether or not you want to bring home some filets. Be sure to read the regulations and understand the requirements ahead of time. You do not want to be leaving Alaska only to find yourself in trouble with the law. Fines can be quite expensive.

CHAPTER SIX

Wildlife

A hungry brown bear collecting his lunch on the Kanektok River.

Bears

Coastal salmon rivers in Alaska are also home to bears, both black and brown bears, with a high concentration of either species in certain locations. You will find bears, or at the very least signs of bear activity, on every Alaska stream or river that supports salmon runs. Black bears in Alaska are the same species, *Ursus americanus,* found throughout Canada and the United States. Brown bears, *Ursus arctos,* are much larger than grizzly bears, *Ursus arctos horribilus,* of inland Alaska, Canada, Montana, and Wyoming. Brown bears attain their great size from genetics and nutrition. Depending on which Alaska wildlife biologist you talk to, brown bears that live within seventy-five to one hundred miles of the coast that have spawning salmon available to them are considered brown bears. The largest of the Alaska brown bears are reputed to be the Kodiak bears. Alaska grizzly bears are a smaller subspecies of brown bears that live further inland. They do not have the annual salmon supply as a part of their diet.

Some bear experts claim that black bears are more unpredictable than brown bears. There is also some evidence that black bears are responsible for more life-threatening situations, possibly because of their shear numbers. I have been fortunate enough to be around both species. I believe that what a person does and the judgment he or she uses will more than likely determine the actions of the bear, whether black or brown. I am referring to two of my favorite words: common sense. If you use common sense in your everyday life you can avoid a lot of problems. This pertains to uninvited encounters with bears as well. All of the black and brown bears that I have encountered in Alaska have been interested in one activity: eating, usually salmon, but in a few instances grasses and berries. We leave them alone and watch from a distance. So far they have reciprocated in kind.

Here are a few common-sense rules to help you avoid dangerous situations with bears:

- Keep a clean camp – burn your garbage thoroughly and dispose of fish entrails in the river. Keep all food, snacks, gum, toothpaste, toiletries out of the tents. Wash dishes immediately after cooking. Store your food away from camp each night.
- Remove any food or snacks and wash off any fish blood from the rafts each evening.
- Leave your dog at home. A dog is nothing but trouble in bear country
- Do not surprise or startle a bear; whistle, talk, shout, and make noise when walking in bear habitat.
- Walk in groups and stay out in the open. Avoid walking in dense brush and stands of trees, Avoid heavily-used bear trails.
- Do not camp within four hundred yards of an outlet of a tributary, this is favorite feeding areas for bears. Do not camp near heavy bear use areas or near where a bear has cached a kill.
- If you see a cub or cubs, leave the area immediately – the sow is nearby. She can get very defensive and angry in short order, and this is the most dangerous kind of bear.
- Do not let a bear see you with a fish on the line; cut the line or get rid of the fish any way you can and slowly back away from the bear.
- Do not sneak up on bears to take photos – stay well away. Use a large telephoto lens instead.
- Stay in the river as much as you can while fishing and be seen. Avoid walking the tall grass river banks, this is where bears walk.
- Try not to panic if you meet a bear up close, above all do not run. Avoid direct eye contact and back away slowly or even stay put, but Talk loudly to the bear and make yourself look as large as possible by holding a pack or log above your head.
- Roll up and play dead if you are attacked by a brown bear. If attacked by a black bear, fight with all your might with whatever you have or can find.

Biting Bugs

Some of Alaska's better-known residents are its biting insects. Unless you are fishing in very cold weather, you will more than likely become acquainted with these pesky critters. Mosquitoes, black flies, and biting midges, better known as no-see-ums, are the bugs to which I am referring.

There are some tricks you can use to reduce the number of attacks by these aerial warriors, which means less collateral damage to your body. Your clothing selection, including colors, is very important. Bugs love dark reds, blacks, and especially navy blue, so try to stay away from these. Take light grays, tans, or neutral colors. Long-sleeve shirts and pants are also important deterrents. They work even better when the cuffs are sealed with tape or Velcro. Consider a head net, but remember that all are not built with the same mesh size. Take a look at www.llbean.com for their Bug Out Headnet, the cost is $12.00.

Your next line of defense is repellants, and there is a multitude from which to choose. Find something that works for you without any side effects or allergic reactions before you head for Alaska. Leave the aerosol repellants home because their spray mechanisms do not always work. DEET is the favorite and the most effective repellant ingredient for slowing down these active pests, but not everyone can use it because of sensitive skin or allergies. The concentration level of DEET in the repellant may be the deciding

This black bear had our prospective campsite reserved for himself.

FLOATING ALASKA! PLANNING SELF-GUIDED FISHING EXPEDITIONS 63

This grizzly has had enough of the Aniak River for now.

factor for you, so find what you think works best with your body. Be super careful when dispensing DEET because the chemicals can deteriorate fly lines as well as some waders. There are some herbal-based repellants available that may do the job. These are probably best for children.

Campfire smoke is also a roadblock to flying pests, but remember that you don't need a roaring blaze to get the job done. A small fire will scatter all but the most determined of biting bugs. You will generally find fewer mosquitoes, black flies, and no-see-ums while you are floating the river than when ashore. And of course a good Alaska breeze is very helpful.

Someone has determined that insects do not like mint; maybe it's the odor or chemical makeup of this plant. It might be worth a try to chew mint-flavored gum or candy or put a little mint on your plate at supper if the insect population gets a little overbearing.

There will still be some of these nasty critters that have the resolve to get through all the armor your arsenal has to offer. They have delivered bites that itch like crazy. This is when you will be glad that you brought along your After Bite-The Itch Eraser or Benadryl Itch Relief Stick. Either of these sticks should be available off the shelf at your local pharmacy.

Biting, flying insects are just a fact of life in the summer days and warmer nights of the Alaska bush. Prepare as best you can, but don't fret about them; you will be OK. You can always hibernate in your tent, but who wants to experience the splendor of Alaska this way.

Wildlife Watching

It is easy to get so content with the fishing that you miss seeing many of the animals that inhabit a riparian ecosystem. Watching the wildlife in their surroundings should be just as important to any avid outdoorsman as the fishing. Time is well spent when observing wildlife because it helps you understand how species interact with each other and the importance of the habitat to these specie relationships. It will teach you why clean air, clean water, and space are so vital to healthy wildlife populations, why man has a responsibility to nature.

A pair of lightweight binoculars such as 8X20s or 10X25s will certainly enhance your wildlife viewing opportunities. The same is true of a small spotting scope mounted on a short, hunting-style tripod. Large mammals such as bears, wolves, or even smaller animals can be seen clearly at some distance with the aid of decent optics.

The bottom line is that the more you look, the more you will see. Birds are common; on occasion bald eagles, can be seen soaring high overhead and mergansers observed almost every day. Cliff swallows and noisy

A grizzly searching for an easy meal.

Wolf tracks.

ravens will most likely be common sights, along with a wide variety of songbirds. Bears can be found feeding on salmon or on hillsides digging for ground squirrels or roots. Moose might be encountered in the willow or alder bottoms or even the marshy areas. Every time you beach the rafts to fish a likely looking run or hole you will see tracks from previous visitors; not the human kind. A small guidebook of animal tracks will help you identify which species left their prints in the mud or sand. With luck you might see fox, wolf, bear, wolverine, and moose tracks all on the same sand bar.

Some rivers have greater wildlife watching potential than others, while sections of the same river are better than other sections. Species and their densities change as habitats differ along a river's course. Caribou may be quite common in the tundra summer range, but are rarely observed towards the lower end of the river. Look for wolves near the caribou herds. Lynx might only be found in the coniferous forest habitat where snowshoe hares are plentiful. Beaver activity is most abundant around alders or willows. Each species has food and habitat requirements for the survival of a population.

All of the animals you will see on your float trip will be wild. Do not expect them to act like zoo animals because even the smaller animals can be dangerous when provoked or misjudged. Leave their young alone! Photograph all species from a distance. Treat all of the fauna and their habitat with respect. Remember that this is their home.

Take the time to look, listen, and learn. It is very satisfying.

CHAPTER SEVEN

Miscellaneous

The Class IV Upper Falls on the Kisaralik is definitely one to portage.

Common Sense and Good Judgment

Wow! What a title! What do these terms mean to you on your Alaska adventure? Are they important?

Let's start with the last question. Suppose you are about three days into a fourteen-day, one hundred-mile fish/float trip that took you almost a year to plan. One of your buddies is seriously injured because he did something stupid. He was mauled by a sow bear, with cubs, after he intentionally got too close to the trio to take photographs. Your group is seventy miles from the nearest town and his life is in serious danger. His poor decision may or may not cost him his life, but either way your group's once-in-a-lifetime trip will most likely be ruined. No one is going to have fun in the days that follow.

Every person in your group must think clearly at all times to avoid accidents or miscalculations. Beach the rafts when you come upon nasty-looking whitewater or log jams. Scout ahead on foot; plan your route. Portage if it is too dangerous for people or the rafts. This will take some time, but at least everyone and the gear will be in one piece, ready again to head down river. Always pull the rafts up on shore and tie them to a boulder or tree to prevent a gust of wind from blowing them down river. You must be especially careful when handling or working with knives, axes, propane stoves, campfires, and boiling water. If you have a gun or two along for protection from bears, DO NOT play with them or even target practice. Always treat firearms as if they were loaded. DO NOT keep a shotgun or rifle loaded in the chamber at any time unless absolutely necessary. Be sure to unload the weapon before its nightly cleaning. A little liquor is OK, but this is neither the time nor the place for a member of your party to get drunk or over indulge. Pinch down the barbs on all hooks. An errant cast with a fly or lure can do some serious damage. A barbless hook is much easier to remove from a part of your body than one with a barb.

Every person in your party must be able to rely on each other to use good common sense and to make sound decisions. A successful trip is measured by more than good fishing. It also involves a relaxing daily routine on the river, camping, hiking, and being able to be around wildlife in such a splendid locale with special friends or family, all while doing it safely. Making wise choices can prevent accidents. Think ahead before you make a decision because each decision will have a consequence. You will want to remember your vacation of a lifetime because of the good times, not because of the bad times.

The scenery is always spectacular on the Aniak River.

Typical Day

There may be no such thing as a typical day on an Alaskan river. Sure there are daily chores to do such as cooking, washing dishes, breaking down camp, packing the rafts, cleaning the campsite, and of course fishing. Beyond this, every day will bring something new because the neat thing about floating a river is that you do not know what you will see around the next bend. There might be an interesting mountain to climb, blueberries to pick, or time taken to observe wildlife in their surroundings.

River fishing is often different from day to day; I guess that's why it's called fishing rather than catching. The upper stretches may be better for arctic char or grayling while salmon numbers increase as you proceed down the river, getting closer to the ocean. Leopard rainbows may be found feeding on roe just below schools of salmon holding in pools or runs or even along the banks. The backwater sloughs might be productive for northern pike or even salmon resting on their way up river to spawn.

Habitats can change as your trip progresses down river. The river's headwaters may be located in the treeless tundra country. A few days of floating might find you drifting through a coniferous forest or alder-lined riverbanks. Permafrost may show itself on eroded riverbanks, with wildflowers, grasses, and berries all a part of the magnificent landscape.

Summer weather in Alaska can change from day to day. Two or more straight days of heavy rain can change some plans or alter your routine. Consecutive sunny days in a row can do the same.

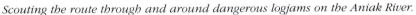

Scouting the route through and around dangerous logjams on the Aniak River.

FLOATING ALASKA! PLANNING SELF-GUIDED FISHING EXPEDITIONS

Kerry Barbero fly-fishing for salmon downstream from Reflection Lake.

You will most likely see terrain changes as you proceed down the river. High rugged mountains, which make for great hiking country, are generally the norm around the lake where your floatplane sets you down. After several days of floating the river you will be out of the mountains, into the foothill country. All too soon you are in the flatter country nearing the river's estuary, close to the end of your voyage. And what a voyage it was!

A Special Morning on the River

Six a.m. and the sunshine has already lit up the inside of my yellow nylon tent, not that it matters much because the August Alaska night never did get totally dark anyway. I should get up and take a leak, but this sleeping bag and pillow feel so darn good. I can't stand it any longer, my bladder surely is not as large as it once was. Oh well! Maybe I can get up without waking everybody else. What a morning! Sunshine, quiet, and calm. A stillness in the air like a rare gem. How lucky am I to be here over a hundred miles from civilization with my friends. Life can't get any better than this, or can it? Blurry eyed, I pick up the shotgun and walk several hundred yards upriver along the sandy river bank to stretch my legs, watching for fresh bear tracks as I go. I take several big breaths to soak in the cool moist air. My eyes are still attempting to focus as I look for bears, wolves, or any other animals on the hillside about one-half mile back up the valley. After five minutes, I haven't seen a thing, just the outstanding scenery.

David Barbero, at left, and the author searching the outlet of Reflection Lake for salmon.

    A movement draws my attention; the back of a fish protrudes from a swirl along the bank on the other side of the river. Could it be a large rainbow? It appeared to be. I stare, but see nothing more of the big fish. Just maybe, with some luck, I can catch him. I hurry back to camp. Without a lot of coordination, I excitedly manage to fumble my way into my chest waders and wading boots. I grab my five-weight Sage, my vest, and go. Hustle back up the gravel bar where I step in to the cool, clear water. Wow, I had better slow down. Might spook it. I ease cautiously across the river, shuffle stepping as I go. Got to stay downstream from where I think he is lurking. Don't want to spook him. He has to be under that branch lying out over the water. Cast as I go, easy does it. Fortunate that I still had the big mouse pattern on from last evening. Smart fish! It is a tough place to get a natural drift. Maybe if I take about three side steps upstream, that will give me a thirty-foot quartering cast. Should be able to drift the mouse under the branch. I make too short a cast, plus there is some line drag. Didn't mend right. I am fishing like a beginner. Excitement doesn't help. I need to calm down; do a better job. Concentrate, think, relax! I cast again. Much better this time, but the fly is still short of its mark. The next cast softly lands the mouse fly on the water about a foot from the grassy bank. The big fly begins its descent to the ocean. Only time for one line mend, the mouse is already drifting lazily under the branch. An unassuming swirl; the fly is gone, as if an underwater vacuum sucked it from the face of the earth. I'm alert and react. I set the hook; the pale green fly line is slicing through the water as the fish heads up stream in a rage. The water explodes as the fish goes airborne from its liquid sanctuary. It's a big rainbow, just as I hoped. I hang on as line rips from my Battenkill disc reel, singing a tune in the early morning Alaska air. Another splendid jump, then another. I can see the big wide crimson stripe down the length of the rainbow's body. The graphite rod is bowed as never before as the big fish charges all over the river. How much pressure do I dare put on the 2X tippet? Time seems to be standing still. Something has to give! It's working. I'm fishing from experience now, getting the upper hand. The big trout's runs aren't as powerful as they first were. I'm gaining line as I carefully back peddle to the shallow shoreline. I am getting better looks at him as his runs become shorter. His runs are less frequent. Finally, after what seemed like an eternity, he is at my feet in about eight inches of water. I admire his beauty as the magnificent leopard rainbow lies motionless in the shallow water, exhausted, or so I think. Slowly I glide my hand down the leader towards the fly, but he reacts. With one sudden burst of energy he lurches for freedom. Quickly he is gone. The mouse fly is dangling from my fly rod that is now straight as an arrow. I stand there, staring in disbelief. Did this really happen to me? No photos, no witness, no sign of the trophy rainbow. How big? Possibly ten or eleven pounds. More likely fourteen or fifteen after my story is told and retold. Who knows for sure?

Public Cabins

An alternative for those who do not think they are up to a self-guided float trip, but who still want the Alaska wilderness experience, is to rent a cabin. Southeast Alaska is the location for nearly two hundred federal cabins designed for public use. Many of these cabins are found in very remote areas with some offering very good fishing opportunities. Any person of at least eighteen years of age may rent one of these for a nightly charge. Fees range from twenty-five to forty-five dollars per night for a cabin, depending on the popularity of the site and the size of the structure. Most of the cabins are small one-room affairs that can handle four people easily while other cabins are two room structures that can accommodate eight or more people. A few of the cabins are even situated near natural hot springs, which of course makes them quite desirable. Some of the popular cabins have restrictive length-of-stay limitations than do others, but all of the cabins have some regulations to which their users must adhere. Each cabin is unique in its location with what it has to offer. A little research is required before you select one.

Southeast Alaska is noted for its rainfall. Even though the cabins do not come fully equipped, they do provide a dry shelter with ample room for comfort. Each cabin is equipped with either an oil or wood-burning stove, table, benches, bunkbeds, and an outhouse. The stove is great for

Kelly Crane and the author in a typical boat the Forest Service provides with many of their rental cabins.

cooking, warming a chilled body or for drying clothes. Some cabins are also supplied with a skiff or small boat, but no motor. However, motors can be used in non-wilderness areas; your floatplane service should be able to assist you in renting a small one. For the most part, these cabins are well maintained, normally by the U.S. Forest Service, and should have been left clean by the previous tenants.

Each cabin has its own personality including recreation potential, fishing, hiking opportunities, wildlife viewing, and scenery. As previously mentioned, some research will be required to choose the cabin that best suits your needs and expectations. Start with www.reserveusa.com on the web to bring up Alaska Cabins. This is the National Recreation Reservation Service. It will give you information on every cabin such as location, cost per night, along with a general description. Familiarize yourself with this web site because it is the easiest way to reserve the cabin you want. Don't wait until the last minute to make your reservation. Many of the popular cabins are booked five or six months in advance. Start your research and planning as much as nine months ahead of time. Call the local district Forest Service office for information on specific cabins. Ask for the person who maintains particular cabins or for those who have direct knowledge of the cabin and the surrounding area. Ask to be sent the USFS booklet pertaining to public-use cabins along with anything else they can send you. You will also need a list of floatplane services for the area. Call the Chamber of Commerce in the nearest town to the cabin. Ask for this list as well as a list of lodging providers in that town. Phone the fisheries biologist with the Alaska Game and Fish Department in the town closest to the cabin in which you are interested. This will be your best source of information concerning salmon runs, timing, trout species, type of water, and the general quality of the fishery. The people you will be on the phone with are happy to help you, but don't pester them on a weekly basis. Write down all your questions, call them once, and then accurately write down their responses.

Several of these cabins are accessible only by saltwater transportation. Southeast Alaska tides are as much as sixteen feet; you must have the tide schedule for the area you will be visiting to determine the best times to boat or fly to the cabin site. You can find this schedule on the Internet. Bring up a search engine such as www.go.com. or www.excite.com. Next enter the Alaska town or city, such as Sitka or Ketchikan, you will use as the point of departure to the USFS cabin. The tide schedule should be readily available along with other pertinent information about that community.

Do not limit your information to one cabin, it may not be available when you want it. Select four, then prioritize them based on what you want and what they have to offer.

Once you make your cabin reservation, it's time to go to the other details such as airline reservations, floatplane reservations, and possibly lodging in town before or after your cabin stay. Consider adding a saltwater fishing charter, especially if this is a once-in-a-lifetime Alaska wilderness vacation. Southeast Alaska is noted for its terrific halibut fishing. Alaska Travelers Accommodations at www.alaskatravelers.com, or 1-800-928-3308, will help you with lodging or charter boat reservations.

David Barbero on the porch of a U.S.F.S. public cabin.

You will need detailed topographical maps that cover several miles in all directions from the cabin. Hiking is fun, but you need to know where you are and where you are going. Order these from the US Geological Service in Denver, Colorado by phoning 1-888-ASK-USGS.

Rain or low clouds can delay your pickup from the cabin. For this reason you will want to have an extra three-days' supply of food for your party. Your group should also try to have flexible time schedules. You could miss an important meeting at work or a family's member wedding because bad weather did not allow the floatplane to pick you up until two days later than planned.

Because the cabins are supplied with bare-bone necessities, you will need to bring the following: ice chest, sleeping bags, sleeping pads, gas or propane cook stove and lantern, fuel, hatchet, small bow saw, all pots, pans, plates utensils, dishwashing tubs, cups, toilet paper, paper towels, matches, army-shovel, water jugs, trash bags, food, water purifier, life jackets, and possibly oil for the heat stove. Propane and fuel oil can usually be purchased where you buy your fishing licenses. In short, do not expect to find anything that is not nailed down. Plan carefully because the floatplanes do have a load capacity.

The next guests after you to use the cabin will appreciate a pile of split, dry firewood, swept floors, and a washed-off table. Leave the cabin in as clean condition as possible; be sure to pack out your trash. Do not bury

Black bears do know how to catch pink salmon.

FLOATING ALASKA! PLANNING SELF-GUIDED FISHING EXPEDITIONS

anything or shove trash down the outhouse vault. These are public cabins that belong to all of us. They must be cared for for future generations to enjoy.

Sample Itinerary

Day 1: Arrive Ketchikan at 11:30 a.m., take taxi into town, eat lunch, buy fishing licenses and necessary groceries, stove/lantern fuel, and ice. Fly out by reserved floatplane to cabin the same afternoon.

Day 2 through 6: Fish, hike, view wildlife, relax, and enjoy your Alaska experience.

Day 7: Pack your gear and clean the cabin. Be ready for a 10:00 a.m. pick-up by the floatplane. Return to Ketchikan. Eat lunch and check into your reserved bed and breakfast or motel. Sightsee and purchase souvenirs.

Day 8: Enjoy half or a full day of saltwater fishing from your reserved charter boat. Stay the night in Ketchikan.

Day 9: Fly home.

Sample Costs for Ketchikan-Area Public Cabin Vacation

The following estimated 2004 expenses are for a six-night stay at a public cabin in the vicinity of Ketchikan to fish in August for salmon and trout. I have selected the Bakewell cabin on the shoreline of Bakewell Lake in the Misty Fiords National Monument for this sample. The following estimated expenses are based on four average-size adults with their gear, which would require the 1200-pound capacity of a Beaver floatplane:

Flight from Seattle to Ketchikan: $392.00/person	$1568.00
Floatplane: deliver & pickup to Bakewell lake	900.00
Cabin Rental for six nights: $35.00/night	210.00
Fishing License for seven days: $30.00/person	120.00
Outboard motor rental for six days: $20.00/day	120.00
Groceries and stove/lantern fuel	275.00
Meals in transit	140.00
Tips to floatplane pilots	120.00
Ketchikan taxi & ferry	65.00
Miscellaneous expenses	200.00
TOTAL	$3718.00

Divide $3718.00 by four. The estimated cost per person would be just under $930.00, plus airfare from your home to Seattle. For an additional $350.00 per person you can add one full day of charter boat fishing for halibut, meals, and two nights stay at a bed and breakfast in Ketchikan.

CHAPTER EIGHT
Sources, Resources & Services

A wheeled version of an Alaska bush taxi.

Commercial Airlines Serving Remote Alaska
Alaska Airlines; www.alaskaair.com; 1-800-252-7522
Era Aviation; www.eraaviation.com; 1-800-866-8394
Frontier Flying Service; www.frontierflying.com; (907) 474-0014
PenAir; www.penair.com; 1-800-448-4226
Yute Air Alaska; www.yuteair.com; (907) 842-5333

Floatplanes, Raft and Camp Gear Rental
Anchorage
Alaska Raft and Kayak – Raft and camp gear rentals – 1-800-606-5950; (907) 561-7238; www.alaskaraftandkayak.com
Alaska Wild Rivers – Raft rentals – (907) 344-9453
Harry O. Brown's Wild Kobuk River Runners – Raft and camp gear rentals – Kobuk, Noatak, & Ambler Rivers; (907) 345-5956; http://home.gci.net/~kobukriver
Katmailand, Inc. – Floatplanes and raft rentals – Alagnak River;1-800-544-0551, (907)-243-5448; www.katmailand.com
Papa Bear Adventures – Floatplanes, raft and camp gear rentals – 1-888-868-8008, (907)-543-2181; www.pbadventures.com
** Also serves Bethel

Aniak
Aniak Air Guides – Floatplanes, raft and camp gear rentals –

(907) 675-4540 in summer; (612) 810-2691 or (612) 414-8876 in winter; www.aniakairguides.com

Inland Aviation – Floatplanes and raft rentals – (907) 675-4624 or (907) 675-4335; www.inlandaviation.com

Bethel

Kuskokwim Wilderness Adventures – Floatplanes, raft and gear rentals – (907) 543-3900 or (907) 543-3239; www.marin.cc.ca.us/~jim/johnmac.html

Bettles

Bettles Lodge & Air Services – Float planes, raft and camp gear rentals –1-800-770-5111, (907) 692-5111; www.akcache.com/bettleslodge .alaska.net/~bttlodge/btlfloat.html

Dillingham

Alaska Adventures – Raft and camp gear rentals – (907) 842-4303 in summer or (507)-835-2596 in winter; www.alaskaoutdoors.com/ARA/

Bay Air – Floatplanes and raft rentals – (907) 842-2570; www.alaskaoutdoors.com/BayAir/index.htm

Float Alaska Raft Rentals Inc. – Raft and camp gear rentals – (907) 842-3400 in summer or (208) 234-2226 in winter;http://members.aol.com/floatak

Freshwater Adventures – Grumman amphibian airplanes and cataraft rentals – (907) 842-5060; www.fresh-h2o.com

Iliamna

Iliamna Air Guides – Floatplanes, raft and camp gear rental – (907) 571-1251; www.airguides.com

Iliamna Air Taxi – Floatplanes and raft rentals – (907) 571-1248; www.arctic.net/~newhalen/IliamnaAirTaxiInc./iliairtaxi.html

Newhalen Rafts, Inc. – Raft rentals – (907) 571-1374; www.arctic.net/~newhalen/NewhalenRafts/NewhalenRafts.html

King Salmon

Branch River Air Service – Floatplanes and raft rentals – (907) 246-3437 in summer or (907) 248-3539 in winter; www.branchriverair.com

King Salmon Guides – Floatplanes, raft and camp gear rentals – Alagnak and Moraine Rivers; (847) 991-6225; www.kingsalmonguides.com

Fishing Information
Alaska Department of Fish and Game
Headquarters in Juneau – (907) 465-4100
www.state.ak.us/local/akpages/FISH.GAME/adfghome.htm

Alaska Department of Fish and Game Division of Sport Fish
Anchorage	(907) 267-2153
Bethel	(907) 543-1677
Cordova	(907) 424-3212 (summer); (907) 267-2415 (winter)
Delta Junction	(907) 895-4632
Dillingham	(907) 842-2427
Douglas	(907) 465-4320
Fairbanks	(907) 459-7216
Glennallen	(907) -822-3309
Haines	(907) 766-3638
Homer	(907) 235-1739
Juneau	(907) 465-4180
Ketchikan	(907) 225-2859
Kodiak	(907) 486-1880
Nome	(907) 443-5796 (summer); (907)-459-7270 (winter)
Palmer	(907) 746-6323
Petersburg	(907) 772-5231
Prince of Wales Island	(907) 755-8802
Sitka	(907) 747-5355
Soldotna	(907) 262-9368
Yakutat	(907) 784-3222

Department of the Interior
Bureau of Land Management Offices
Anchorage District Office	(907) 267-1225
Anchorage Field Office	(907) 267-1246
Arctic District Office - Fairbanks	(907) 474-2301
Glennallen District Office	(907) 822-3217
Kobuk District Office – Fairbanks	(907) 474-2343
Kotzebue Field Office	(907) 442-2720
Nome Field Office	(907) 443-2177
Northern District Office – Fairbanks	(907) 474-2200
State Office – Anchorage	(907) 271-5960 or (907) 271-5555
Steese/White Mountains District Office – Fairbanks	(907) 474-2350
Tok Field Office	(907) 883-5121

U.S. Fish and Wildlife Service
National Wildlife Refuges
Arctic National Wildlife Refuge – Fairbanks	(907) 456-0250
Alaska Peninsula/Becharof NWR Complex– King Salmon	(907) 246-3339
Innoko National Wildlife Refuge – McGrath	(907) 524-3251
Izembek National Wildlife Refuge – Cold Bay	(907) 532-2445
Kanuti National Wildlife Refuge – Fairbanks	(907) 456-0329
Kenai National Wildlife Refuge – Soldotna	(907) 262-7021
Kodiak National Wildlife Refuge – Kodiak	(907) 487-2600
Koyukuk/Nowitna NWR Complex – Galena	(907) 656-1231
Selawik National Wildlife Refuge – Kotzebue	(907) 442-3799
Tetlin National Wildlife Refuge – Tok	(907) 883-5312
Togiak National Wildlife Refuge – Dillingham	(907) 842-1063
Yukon Delta National Wildlife Refuge – Bethel	(907) 543-3151
Yukon Flats National Wildlife Refuge – Fairbanks	(907) 456-0440

National Forests of Alaska Public Recreation Cabin Information
U.S. Forest Service Ranger Districts
Cordova	(907) 424-7661
Craig	(907) 826-3271
Glacier	(907) 783-3242
Hoonah	(907) 945-3631
Juneau	(907) 586-8800
Ketchikan	(907) 225-2148
Petersburg	(907) 772-3871
Seward	(907) 224-3374
Sitka	(907) 747-4220
Thorne Bay	(907) 828-3304 or 3305
Wrangell	(907) 874-2323
Yakutat	(907) 784-3359

Public Cabin Reservations
National Recreation Reservation Service 1-877-444-6777
www.reserveusa.com

Additional Public Cabin Information
Southeast Alaska Discovery Center – (907) 228-6214
www.fs.fed.us/r10/tongass/districts/discoverycenter/

More Excellent Books for Alaska!

ALASKA FISHING ON A BUDGET
Bernard R. Rosenberg

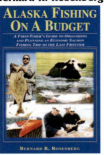

SB: $14.95
ISBN: 1-57188-297-9

FLY PATTERNS OF ALASKA
Alaska Flyfishers
(Revised and enlarged edition)

SB: $19.95
ISBN: 1-878175-31-9

DRY FLY FISHING
Dave Hughes

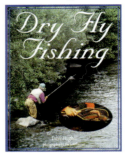

SB: $15.95
ISBN: 1-878175-68-8

SPINNER FISHING FOR STEELHEAD, SALMON & TROUT
Jed Davis

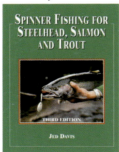

SB: $19.95
ISBN: 0-936608-40-4

DRIFT BOAT FLY FISHING
A River Guide's Sage Advice
Neale Streeks

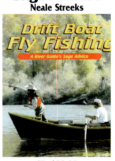

SB: $29.95
ISBN: 1-57188-016-X

NYMPH FISHING
Dave Hughes

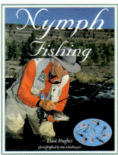

SB: $19.95
ISBN: 1-57188-002-X

ALASKA RAINBOWS
Larry Tullis

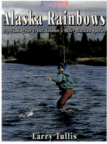

(AK) ISBN: 1-57188-251-0
SB: 19.95
(AK) ISBN: 1-57188-274-X
HB: 30.00

Ask for these books at your local fly/tackle shop or call toll-free to order:
1-800-541-9498 (8 to 5 p.s.t.) • www.amatobooks.com
Frank Amato Publications, Inc. • P.O. Box 82112 • Portland, Oregon 97282